An Unauthorized History of the RCMP

An Unauthorized History of the RCMP

Lorne and Caroline Brown

James Lewis & Samuel
Toronto
1973

ISBN 0-88862-035-7 (cloth)
     0-88862-036-5 (paper)

Design by Lynn Campbell
Cover design by Christer Themptander
Cover photo: Jorgen Halling, The Canadian Magazine

James Lewis & Samuel, Publishers
Toronto

Printed and bound in Canada

Contents

Acknowledgements

We obtained many of our source materials from the Public Archives of Canada, the Archives of Saskatchewan and the Library of the University of Saskatchewan, Regina Campus. The Metis Society of Saskatchewan also assisted us with information and allowed us complete access to their files.

We have made considerable use of secondary sources as readers will see by the notes at the conclusion of chapters. We wish to acknowledge three unpublished M.A. theses which were of particular value to us. They are: Stanley D. Hanson, *The Estevan Strike and Riot, 1931,* Regina Campus, 1971; E. C. Morgan, *The North-West Mounted Police, 1873-1883,* Regina Campus, 1970; and W. P. Ward, *Administration of Justice in the North-West Territories, 1870-87,* University of Alberta, Edmonton, 1966.

We have received invaluable assistance from dozens of people many of whom cannot be named. We will therefore express our thanks to all of them collectively rather than mentioning any by name. Without these people the writing of this book would not have been possible.

Caroline A. Brown
Lorne A. Brown

Introduction

During 1973, the centennial year of the Royal Canadian Mounted Police, Canadians will read and hear a great deal about their federal police force. Most of the speeches, television programs and newspaper accounts will portray the RCMP as the time-honoured epitome of an honest and efficient police force rendering, without fear or favour, the type of service and protection befitting the citizens of a democratic society. For two reasons, most people will not question this image. First, Canadians (and everybody else) like to view themselves and their institutions in a positive light. And second, the average Canadian has very little actual contact with the RCMP.

Most books about the RCMP approach the subject from the romantic "good versus evil" perspective of Western movies and TV police dramas — the incorruptible Force in a perpetual struggle against evil lawbreakers. Few of these books deal with the Force realistically, nor do they attempt to question issues fundamental to the history, ideology and activities of the RCMP, such as: Were the Mounted Police established by the federal government, as is popularly supposed, mainly because government leaders in Ottawa wished to protect the Indian population of the Northwest from the depredations of whiskey traders and other outlaws, or were there less altruistic reasons? Why, after Western Canada was organized into provinces, were the Royal Northwest Mounted Police retained as a highly centralized federal force? Why was their jurisdiction eventually extended throughout Canada when they became the Royal Canadian Mounted Police? Have the RCMP played a neutral or a consistently biased role in industrial and political disputes in Canada? Are the Mounted Police regarded with the same reverence by minority groups such as Indians and Metis as they are by white middle-class Canadians, and if not why not? Why have the RCMP always been so secretive? Is the existence of a highly centralized police force of a military character a threat or a potential threat to the liberty of Canadians?

1

What are the actual opinions of top-ranking RCMP officers about racial and ethnic minorities, organized labour, youthful dissenters and other groups in our society?

In this book, we have attempted to provide answers or at least partial answers to just these questions as a modest beginning toward an understanding of what the RCMP are really like. Because we approach the subject from this perspective, we do not deal extensively with the day-to-day policing duties of the RCMP. Rather we address ourselves to examining the origins and some aspects of the early history of the Force. We also examine the role of the modern RCMP in relation to industrial conflict and urban unrest in Canada. Most of the emphasis here is on the period between the two wars, which was a period of considerable turmoil in Canada. We attempt to explain the ideology of the RCMP and the extent to which they have performed an explicitly political role in Canadian affairs. One chapter deals in a general way with the relationship between the modern RCMP and minority groups in Canada and two chapters examine in detail specific cases of RCMP involvement with people of Indian ancestry. We also attempt to explain the process by which the RCMP gained such a positive image among Canadians and then consider to what extent that image is justified.

Our survey concentrates more on Western Canada than on the rest of the country, partly because we are Westerners with access to Western source materials and are more familiar with the West than with the rest of the country, but mainly because of the importance of the West to the RCMP themselves. The original Force was founded for the purpose of occupying the Northwest as the policing instrument of the federal government, and its jurisdiction was limited to what later became the Western provinces and the North. Even after the creation of the modern RCMP in 1920 and the extension of jurisdiction throughout the country, many of those Mounted Police activities which we discuss were more concentrated in the West than elsewhere. There seems to have been more overt industrial conflict in the West than in central Canada in the period between the world wars, and much of what did occur in Ontario and Quebec was handled by provincial police forces. To this day the RCMP are a much more pervasive force in the Western provinces than in Ontario and Quebec because of the fact that in the West they act as provincial and often municipal police as well as being the direct arm of the federal government.

We also concentrate on English Canada. Apart from the difficulty of access to source materials in Quebec, Quebec governments have generally distrusted the federal authorities and consequently depended as much as possible upon provincial and municipal police forces. This is not to say that the RCMP are not a presence in Quebec or that the federal government is not willing to intervene in Quebec affairs with massive physical force, as it demonstrated with the implementation of the War Measures Act in October 1970. However, the topic of the RCMP in Quebec we leave to critics in that province.

Any realistic discussion of the historic and contemporary role of the RCMP should be preceded by a brief account of the nature of the organizational structure of the Force. The structural nature of the RCMP has helped to determine both what they have been used for and the outlook of the leading officers of the Force.

The original North West Mounted Police (later the Royal NWMP) were specifically designed to be a para-military cavalry force which would perform not only a conventional police role but which might also be called upon to carry out distinctly military functions. Nearly all of the top officers of the original Force had previous military careers, and they tended to emphasize the military nature of the Force.

When the RNWMP were amalgamated with the old Dominion Police to form the RCMP in 1920, the military nature of the new force was kept intact despite some difficulties in accustoming former civilians to accepting military discipline. The report of the RCMP for the year ending September 30, 1920, makes reference to some of these difficulties to point out how the Mounties differed from other police forces:

> The absorption of the Dominion Police into the Mounted Police was not free from difficulties. Their organization differed fundamentally. The former was organized and uniformed on the lines of a municipal police force, free to resign on short notice, and its discipline enforced by the civil courts. The latter was organized on military lines, its officers commissioned, clothed in scarlet, disciplined under powers conferred by its own Act, and engaged for a fixed term of service, which could not be terminated at will.[1]

The number of leading RCMP personnel who had formerly been associated with the military helped to assure that the Force would remain military in nature. In fact the majority of commissioners since the founding of the Force have either come to the RCMP directly from a military career or received military training prior to involvement with the Force. Those coming directly from a military career included: Lt. Col. A. G. French, Lt. Col. A. G. Irvine, Lt. Col. J. F. Macleod, Major-General J. H. MacBrien and Lieutenant Courtlandt Starnes. Commissioners Perry, Wood and Herchmer had all trained as military officers, the first two at Royal Military College, prior to their association with the RCMP.

An examination of the RCMP Act and is regulations demonstrates that the Force continues to be very much a military organization today. Under the authority of the act, the commissioner is given the power to "make rules, to be known as standing orders, for the organization, training, discipline, efficiency, administration and good government of the Force."[2] Though in theory the authority of the commissioner is subject to the approval of the minister responsible for the RCMP, in practice the minister has no channel of communication with members of the Force other than through the commissioner. The commissioner thus has at least as much authority over his officers and men as a general in the armed forces, if not more.

Like regular military organizations, the RCMP has an elaborate system of rank which is enforced by a rigid obedience to authority. Part II of the act, relating to discipline within the force, indicates that it is a major service offence for a member to "disobey or refuse to obey the lawful command of ... any other member who is his superior in rank or is in authority over him."[3] All offences against regulations are handled as internal matters not subject to civilian courts. Members found guilty of a major service offence before an internal tribunal can be sentenced to significant terms of imprisonment. In fact the act gives the commissioner the authority to imprison RCMP members for up to 30 days without trial and before the matter is brought to the attention of the minister.[4]

Other aspects of the RCMP also reveal its military character. Members who enlist are required to sign up for five years and are not allowed to leave until their term expires except under very special circumstances. A member who deserts the

Force is subject to the disciplinary provisions of the RCMP Act "for a further perior of two years after the expiration of his period of engagement, or, if he left Canada after the desertion and within either of those periods for a period of two years after his return to Canada."[5] The training is military in nature; recruits are housed in barracks and shut off from all normal contact with the public for a period of six months. Members are forbidden to belong to anything resembling a union and grievances can be taken up only by individuals with superior officers and without appeal to any outside authority. Anyone who attempted to take complaints over the head of his commanding officer would quickly find life intolerable, and Part II, Section 25, Sub-section (j) of the RCMP Act stipulates that it is a major service offence for a member to make "an anonymous complaint to the Commissioner or to the Government of Canada or any province or any department thereof, or to any Minister of the Crown or member of Parliament or a provincial legislature."[6] Only recently has a very ineffective grievance procedure been initiated by Commissioner W. L. Higgitt in response to pressure resulting from ex-Corporal Jack Ramsay's exposé of the RCMP in *Maclean's* in July 1972.

The RCMP is also secretive in its operations and takes precautions to see that only officially authorized information about the internal workings of the Force reaches the public. Commissioner's Standing Order No. 1156 (34) states that:

A member shall not: (34) give information of any kind concerning the work or administration of the Force, or any department of the federal or provincial government to the public, by radio, television, an address to a gathering, or by any other medium of communication, without the permission of the Commanding Officer or Officer Commanding; the application for such permission to be accompanied by a short summary of remarks to be made.

We have attempted only a brief survey of some of the above-mentioned aspects of the RCMP. Many of the topics touched upon in this volume, such as the relationship of the Mounted Police to people of Indian ancestry and the role of the Force in labour disputes, merit at least a volume in themselves. The whole story of the RCMP may never be known, given the secrecy with which the Force has always been and continues to be shrouded. However, we have tried to scratch the surface;

hopefully others will examine particular aspects of the subject in greater depth, until perhaps some day Canadians will arrive at a more realistic understanding of the role of the RCMP in our society than most people appear to have at the present time.

Chapter 1
Opening up the West

The officially sanctioned mythology surrounding the origins of the North West Mounted Police (NWMP) is well known to most Canadians and is probably accepted at face value by the majority of them. No wonder: our teachers present it to our children as factual history, the opinion-makers in our governments and mass media go on perpetuating it every day, and the present RCMP cultivate it as ardently as their predecessors ever did, especially as they prepare to celebrate the centennial of the Force in 1973.

The central theme of the myth is that a benevolent government created the North West Mounted Police to protect the Indians from white whiskey traders and swindlers and to ensure that all the people of the Canadian North West — Indians and Metis, settlers and traders — might have the opportunity of living under a system of law impartially enforced and guaranteeing equal rights to all. According to the popular wisdom it was the creation and subsequent performance of the NWMP which prevented Western Canada from developing into a replica of the American West, where the Indians were mercilessly wiped out and the law of the fast gun and the lynch mob prevailed as a substitute for an equitable and orderly system of justice.

This glorification of the Force has been one of the most popular topics chosen by schoolchildren who compete in oratorical contests. The subject is not, however, limited to orations by schoolchildren, but forms the main theme of political speeches and newspaper editorials during most ceremonial occasions relating to Western Canadian history. It also permeates most of what passes for adult literature on the history of the Mounted Police. A typical example of such literature is *Policing the Plains* by R. G. Macbeth, published in 1921, revised in 1931, and for two decades considered one of the standard reference works on the Force.[1] This book extolls the role of the federal government (particularly the NWMP) in settling and building the West, and also pays considerable tribute to the Canadian Pacific Railway. Macbeth presents westward expansion as a great "civilizing" mission and dismisses, often in racist terms, those who objected to the course of events as standing in the way of "progress." He sees the NWMP as indispensable instruments in the march of civilization, as a Force that could do no wrong.

> They have patrolled and guarded and guided this whole North-West Country for the last forty years and more. During that period they have built up a great tradition which rests on a solid foundation of achievement. Their reputation for courage is unchallenged, their record for giving every man of whatever race or colour a square deal is unique, their inflexible determination to see that the law is enforced is well known and their refusal to count the odds against them when duty is to be done has been absolutely proven again and again.[2]

More recent histories of the Force have been less childish, but the theme has remained the same.

An even more absurd way of interpreting historical events, and a favourite of editorialists and the RCMP themselves, is to view them in the context of the extent to which they contributed to the "great tradition" of the Mounted Police. One example occurs in an article that appeared in the Prince Albert *Daily Herald* (and was later reprinted in the *RCMP Quarterly*) on the occasion of the dedication of Batoche Museum by Prime Minister John Diefenbaker in 1961:

> Riel's life proved a strange contrast of good and evil. In his role as rebel leader and inciter of the Metis and Indians he caused many innocent people to lose their lives. But in that role also, he was mainly responsible for the unsettled conditions which led to the founding of the Force now famous the world over for efficiency in enforcing the law.[3]

That the territory now comprising the Prairie provinces was acquired by Canada and peopled by settlers for altruistic reasons is, of course, too absurd an assumption be bear serious examination today. Canadian historians generally agree that an extremely important if not the most important reason for Confederation in 1867 was to serve the needs of the commercial and industrial interests centred in Toronto and Montreal with connections in London. In order to prosper and expand, these companies needed enlarged markets for both primary and manufactured products and, especially in the case of railway and other transportation interests, assurance that trade goods would reach their destination by way of the St. Lawrence route. That the politicians of the day were intimately connected to the business interests has been amply documented by historians and other writers.[4] The first task of the politicians was to unite Ontario, Quebec, New Brunswick and Nova Scotia into the Dominion of Canada. However, in 1867 they already had their eye on British Columbia and Rupert's Land, which was administered by the Hudson's Bay Company under a charter from the British Crown. Shortly after Confederation the federal government began negotiations with the Hudson's Bay Company and Great Britain for the transfer of Rupert's Land to Canada. They also began negotiations to bring British Columbia into Confederation. The idea was to acquire political control to the Pacific and then proceed with the construction of a trans-continental railway. This would presumably encourage an influx of settlers, who would provide a market for the manufactured products of central Canada and business for the transportation interests. A developing West would also provide a lucrative field for in-investment and speculation in grain, timber, minerals and land.

The negotiations with Great Britain and the Hudson's Bay Company were completed in 1869 and arrangements were made to turn Rupert's Land over to the Canadian government. No one consulted the inhabitants of the territory about the transfer of sovereignty or even informed them of what the new order would entail. The plan was to administer the entire North West as a colony of Canada with a governor and council appointed by the federal government. There was not even to be a pretense of self-government; any rights accorded to the inhabitants of the colony would be by the grace and the discretion of the federal government. Not suprisingly the inhabitants, particularly the Metis in the Red River vicinity, objected to this high-handed arrogance. When their objections were ignored, they took up arms and declared a provisional government under the leadership of Louis Riel. Riel and his followers compelled the federal government to negotiate the terms of transfer to Canadian sovereignty, and the result was the Manitoba Act of 1870. Under the terms of the Manitoba Act, the Metis were guaranteed certain linguistic, religious, and territorial rights and the area around Red River was accorded provincial status. It has since been generally conceded that if any one man could be described as the founder of Manitoba it would be Louis Riel.

The province of Manitoba in 1870 was much smaller in area than it is today, and the territory outside the new province, comprising the area now included in the three Prairie provinces, remained a colony of Canada to be administered directly from Ottawa. The inhabitants of what became known as the North West Territories, consisting mainly of Indians, were not consulted any more than their counterparts in Red River had been prior to their resort to arms in 1869.

British Columbia was shortly brought into Confederation as a province and plans were laid for a transcontinental railway to the Pacific and the agricultural settlement of the Prairie West. Eventually much of the best land and many of the most valuable timber and mineral resources were to be turned over to the CPR and other corporations as part of the scheme for colonizing the West. To make the whole scheme a success, financiers and politicians considered it necessary to wrest control of the prairies from the Indian tribes and to compel the Indians to live on "reservations." That is where the NWMP came into the picture. The NWMP were established as a semi-military force designed to keep order on the prairies and to facilitate the transfer of most of the territory of the region from the Indian tribes to the federal government with a minimum of expense and bloodshed.

Most people assume that the NWMP were founded in response to the Cypress Hills Massacre, when American whiskey traders murdered several Assiniboine Indians in May 1873. This is true only in the sense that the massacre hastened the organization of the Force. The establishment of the Force had been planned and officially authorized prior to this, and the primary reason for establishing it was to control the Indian and Metis population of the North West.[5] The apprehension of whiskey traders and other white outlaws was definitely considered of secondary importance and was thought essential mainly because if such people were not controlled they might provoke drastic action by the Indians themselves which would discourage settlement and investment.[6]

S. W. Horrall has pointed out in a recent article in the *Canadian Historical Review* that John A. Macdonald had been making plans for policing the North West since 1869, and that his main concern was to keep peace between Indians and settlers so as to encourage economic development.[7]

Lieutenant-Governor William McDougall, appointed by Macdonald to administer the North West, had plans for such a force when he proceeded to Red River in 1869, and it was the fear of how he would use it which helped to provoke Louis Riel and his followers into taking up arms. The force was to be military in nature and based on the Irish Constabulary, which Great Britain used to control Ireland. Horrall points out that the Irish Constabulary was centrally controlled and "had developed against the background of social unrest and civil strife which was a common feature of nineteenth century Ireland."[8] The plans for this force were approved by an Order-in-Council on April 6, 1870, and Captain D. R. Cameron, an officer of the Royal Artillery, was appointed Commissioner. Cameron would be directly responsible to the federal government and to the Territorial Council. Cameron had specific instructions to make the force multi-racial, an apparent attempt by the government to copy the British colonial authorities in India. "To Macdonald the problem of policing the Northwest resembled that faced by the British in India."[9] Not yet a fully self-governing country herself, Canada was embarking upon imperialist adventures of her own and learning quickly from the undisputed master of the trade.

Cameron's police force was to march west with the Canadian military in 1870, but when the Canadian government was forced to pass the Manitoba Act, which left the administration of justice in the hands of the province, this plan was shelved. The authorities decided that the military would constitute a sufficient federal presence for the time being. However, plans continued for controlling that part of the North West outside of the new province of Manitoba. In the autumn of 1870, A. G. Archibald, lieutenant-governor of Manitoba and *ex officio* governor of the North West Territories, despatched Captain W. F. Butler to the North West to reconnoiter the situation and make recommendations for consolidating control of the area. Butler recommended that the Indian titles to the land be extinguished by treaty, a police force be organized and a commissioner be appointed after the mode of administration in Ireland and India.[10]

No immediate action was taken on Butler's report, but pressure on the federal government to establish a police or military force for the North West mounted during the next couple of years. Many government officials feared that the Metis of Manitoba would ally themselves with the Indian tribes farther west and make another stand against the federal government. The Indians feared that their way of life would be destroyed and their lands wrested from them, and many of them talked of the need to take action against the white intruders before it was too late. In a letter to the secretary of state for the provinces in 1872, Lieutenant-Governor Archibald warned of unrest among the Indians typified by "their increasing tendency to insubordination and insolence," and insisted that this "general feeling of uneasiness . . . contains the elements of much danger."[11] Archibald warned that there was also danger from the Metis of Manitoba and the North West, and insisted, "you must raise a military force to control these elements."[12]

The government appointed Colonel P. Robertson-Ross, commanding officer of the Canadian Militia, to make another survey of the situation in 1872. In his report, Robertson-Ross also called for the formation of an armed force and made reference to the need to guarantee the safety of those who would be building the CPR. While Robertson-Ross mentioned the danger from the liquor traffic and horse thieves, it was clear whom the force would be mainly designed to control: "It should be borne in mind too, that in addition to the Indian element, there is a half-breed population of about 2,000 souls in the Saskatchewan unaccustomed to the restraint of any Government, mainly depending as yet upon the chase for subsistence, and requiring to be controlled nearly as much as the Indian."[13]

Others were also warning the government that their plans for colonizing the West would not come to fruition without the despatch of an armed force. Administrator McKeagney of Government House, For Gary, issued such a warning to John A. Macdonald on May 1, 1873:

> I feel justified in saying that the presence of a military force in the North West is absolutely necessary. Not only shall we fail to attract Immigration to the North West, unless the due protection of Immigrants is thus ensured, but settlers now residing on the frontiers of Manitoba, will through fear of Indian hostilities be induced to leave the Province.[14]

There were also a few people who pointed out to the federal government that the better the Indians were treated the less chance there would be of bloodshed. Dr. John Shultz, M.P., claimed in the House of Commons that the Hudson's Bay

Company was partly responsible for the unrest in the North West because the company had received such a large amount of its lands when Rupert's Land was transferred to Canada whereas Indians covered by a treaty negotiated in 1871 had received only three dollars each per annum.[15] People were to discover in later years that the plunder engaged in by the CPR made the Hudson's Bay Company look like small-time swindlers by comparison.

The government officially established the North West Mounted Police by an Act of Parliament in the spring of 1873. It was to be a semi-military body directly controlled from Ottawa and not by the local government officials in the North West. No special provisions were made for including Indians or Metis in the force as had been suggested in the original plan of 1867. Apparently the events of the so-called Red River Rebellion and the unrest following it had convinced the authorities that the native peoples were not likely to become loyal servants of their colonial masters.

Though the force was officially established in May 1872, it was not intended to be organized and sent into the field until 1874. The Cypress Hills Massacre, perpetrated a few days after Macdonald served notice in the Commons of a proposed bill to establish the NWMP, led to an increased state of unrest in the West which caused the government to speed up its plans. Alexander Morris, the new lieutenant governor of Manitoba and *ex officio* governor of the North West Territories, feared that the outrage in the Cypress Hills and other atrocities of this nature might provoke the Indians into open warfare against the whites. Morris and others increased the pressure for government action. Sir Alexander Campbell, minister of the interior, assured Morris that he had recommended to the Cabinet the sending out of a force as quickly as possible. In doing so Campbell revealed what was uppermost in his mind: "My recommendation was based more upon my appreciation of the impression that such an expedition would exercise upon the minds of the Black Feet than even upon the necessity of removing the band of desperadoes who are doing so much to demoralize the Indians according to the reports you send me."[16] In a letter to Governor-General Dufferin about a month later, John A. Macdonald revealed that the unrest stemmed not only from events in the Cypress Hills but also from continued persecution of some of the activists in the provisional government of 1869-70:

The massacre of the Indians by the Americans has greatly excited the red men there. Added to the other troubles the arrest of Lepine and the consequent flight of Riel from the country has rearoused the fanaticism of the French Canadian Half-breeds and Morris fears all kinds of trouble.[17]

So the despatch of the NWMP to the Western plains was at least partly related to suppressing whiskey traders and preventing recurrences of events like the Cypress Hills Massacre, but obviously not from altruistic motives. What the government feared most was an Indian war over the instrusion of whites from outside the area. Such a war would have been extremely costly to the authorities and could have delayed settlement, railway construction and economic development for many years. There was even the outside possibility of some form of American intervention should such a war continue for any length of time. But above all, such a war had the potential of completely shattering the schemes of the federal politicians and their allies in the business circles of central Canada.

The North West Mounted Police were designed to be a semi-military organization rather than a civilian police force of the conventional type. This early military form of organization continued in later years and is still maintained in the modern RCMP, with undesirable consequences for members of the Force themselves and those members of the public with whom they come in contact in the course of their duties. George Arthur French, a personal friend of John A. Macdonald and a captain in the Royal Artillery, became the first commissioner with the honorary military rank of lieutenant-colonel. French, who was familiar with the Royal Irish Constabulary, proceeded to pattern the Force on military models. Officers under French received honorary military titles and in the early years nearly all of the top officers of the Force, including the first three commissioners, had previous military service, as had many of the men. Of the approximately 300 men who set out from Dufferin, Manitoba, on the march west in 1874, 41 had served in the Regular Service, 14 in the Royal Irish Constabulary, 32 in the Canadian Artillery, and 87 in the Canadian Militia.[18] However, many of the men seem to have objected to the tight military regime imposed by French and other officials and this, along with the severe hardships to which they were subjected, led to widespread desertion during the first few years. The force, in fact, seemed to be plagued with morale problems due to the tyranny of senior officers that ex-RCMP Corporal Jack Ramsay has described as still existing in the RCMP.[19] The Manitoba *Free Press* once described French as "the would-be autocrat of the North-West Mounted Police" and "the sour despot who is not only hated by his own Force, but by others also."[20] Commissioner French was dismissed on July 22, 1876 by Order-in-Council, on the grounds that the state of the Force was unsatisfactory. Clearly, however, political partisanship was also involved for, as a result of the Pacific Scandal of 1873, the Liberals under Alexander Mackenzie had defeated the Macdonald government.[21]

That there were "unsatisfactory" aspects to the Force as early as 1876 has been documented by E. C. Morgan, W. P. Ward and others.[22] The desertion rate had reached epidemic proportions. By 1875 more than half of the 150 original recruits of 1873 had left the Force. Thirty-one men had deserted before the Force ever left Dufferin, Manitoba, in the spring of 1874. Poor food, deplorable living conditions, long delays in receiving wages, and the bullying of officers all played their part in encouraging desertion. The annual report of the NWMP for 1882 attempted to explain the high desertion rate by saying that some of the newer members of the Force had too much concern for their friends or refused to obey rules and regulations.

> A large number of undisciplined men, associated together for a considerable length of time, naturally formed intimacies which were objectionable, for on arrival at the post they thus formed a distinct "clique", apart from the older men. The change of life which they experienced, their surroundings, the discipline, the arduous duties they were called upon to perform, gave rise to *imaginary grievances*, which were nursed and talked over among themselves; not mixing up with the older hands, who would otherwise have imparted a desirable influence, they became dissatisfied.[23] [Italics added]

At first punishments for breaches of discipline consisted only of fines or dismissal from the Force, but soon officials complained that punishments should be stiffer and deserters imprisoned, because they were tarnishing the image of the Force. "Owing to false statements as regards the Force made by a great number of the deserters, and persons not favourable to

it, there appears to be a feeling in favour of the deserters."[24]
The penalty for desertion rose in 1875 to six months' imprisonment, and again in 1882 to one year's imprisonment. A system of rewards for the apprehension of deserters also went into effect. In 1880, Commissioner J. J. Macleod, who had succeeded French in 1876, was succeeded in turn by A. G. Irvine. "Macdonald expressed a conviction that Irvine would improve the Force's efficiency because he had more of the martinet about him."[25]

Internal mismanagement and dissatisfaction sometimes drove the men to the point of organized protest and virtual mutiny. Turner's official history of the NWMP describes one serious disruption at Edmonton in 1886. Dissatisfied with filthy living conditions and promotion procedures, the men engaged in mass insubordination by refusing to carry out orders. A detail of NWMP promptly arrived from headquarters at Regina to arrest the ringleaders. They sentenced six men to prison terms at Regina and dismissed them from the Force. Alcholism, open dissension between officers and men, and a high percentage of personnel suffering from venereal disease were further problems that plagued the Force. In 1880 Mr. Royal, M.P. for Provencher, Manitoba, reported complaints of quarrels between officers and men over women and of sexual exploitation of Indian women.[26] Prostitution was rampant in the vicinity of NWMP forts and there were complaints that the police were spreading venereal disease among the Indians.[27]

Complaints both from within and outside the NWMP increased in the 1880s to the point where they became a public scandal. Police officers complained of a "system of terrorism" within the Force which compelled members to remain silent about their grievances.[28] There were charges of favouritism and tampering with private mail. There were charges of corruption involving government officials, NWMP officers, and corporations including the Hudson's Bay Company, which supplied provisions to the Force. Charges against officers for negligence were frequent. "It is about time that officers in this outfit confined themselves exclusively to their duties as such, and left the management of horse and cattle ranches, coal mines, ferry boats, bogus horse sales, chasing half-breeds all over the Northwest with Government horses after land scrip, to those who are not fortunate enough to hold commissions in this force."[29]

In the late 1880s matters got even worse under Commissioner L. W. Herchmer, who had no previous police experience but who apparently was a favourite with government officials. The situation deteriorated to the point where in 1891 the government was compelled to appoint Hon. Edward Wetmore, a judge of the Supreme Court of the North West Territories, to investigate complaints.[30] There were 137 charges against the commissioner and several more against his brother, Assistant Commissioner W. M. Herchmer, but the latter died and the charges against him were dropped. Charges against the commissioner included interfering with members of the force in their capacities of justices of the peace, influencing officers to oppose a particular candidate in a federal election, acting with injustice, tyranny, ill-temper and cruelty towards members of the Force, travelling on railway passes and then charging the public for the price of the fare, falsifying reports and lying to the government about individual officers, punishing an inspector by sending him to an inferior post after he had given evidence against Herchmer, spying on district officers, and illegally sentencing constables to bread and water diets and solitary confinement.[31] Wetmore's report was to some extent a whitewash in that he interpreted his terms of reference very narrowly and declined to enquire into any matters that could be tried before a court of justice (which included some of the more serious charges). Wetmore did, however, find many of the charges against Herchmer accurate, including arrogant behaviour towards officers and men, the use of bread and water diets, recriminations against critics within the Force, and general humiliation of those serving under him. He also conceded that the commissioner "had used his authority for purposes it was never intended to be used, but that there were faults on both sides."[32] There is no record that Herchmer was tried in the courts for any of the charges which Wetmore declined to enquire into. Nor was he removed as commissioner, a post he held until 1900.

Many of the complaints against the NWMP by the civilian population stemmed from the fact that federal legislation gave the police sweeping powers in the North West Territories which did not exist in the provinces. The NWMP Act of 1873 provided for magistrates and justices of the peace as well, and stipulated that these positions could be filled by members of the Force. In fact there were many instances in the first few years where the same police officers could arrest, prosecute, judge and jail an accused and where there was no appeal procedure.[33] One of the first two magistrates appointed in 1876 was James F. Macleod who also happened to be assistant commissioner and later commissioner of the NWMP. Such duplication of roles became a common practice, which led to much public criticism. The *Prince Albert Times* of March 21, 1884 described the practice as "monstrous, extraordinary, abnormal and utterly unconstitutional.[34] In 1884 and 1885 irate citizens in Calgary called public meetings to object to the practice of police officers serving as magistrates. Gradually the practice stopped.

The administration of justice in general was to a very considerable extent politically motivated in the North West Territories. G. A. French, son of the first commissioner, wrote about how his father's problems in running the Force were intensified by "political appointments without regard to ability or suitability, and constant wire pulling from Ottawa."[35] L. W. Herchmer, himself probably a political appointee, was charged in 1891 (along with 136 other things) of meddling in politics. Magistrates were even more politically motivated than police officers, and some proved so unsuitable that the government had to remove their own appointees due to public pressure. Magistrates held office "during pleasure" rather than "during good behaviour," and so the government was able to exert fairly direct influence over them. One evidence of this influence is a letter from John A. Macdonald to Lieutenant Governor Dewdney in 1885 suggesting that he convey to the magistrates Macdonald's opinion that lengthy sentences should be meted out to the leaders of the Saskatchewan Rebellion.[36] Another is the fact that Hugh Richardson, the stipendiary magistrate before whom Louis Riel was tried for high treason, was also legal advisor to the territorial governor and had shown his prejudice in a letter to the minister of the interior in 1880 in which he described the Metis leadership as "evil influences."[37]

The people of the North West who had most dealings with the NWMP during the first few years were the Indians and Metis. W. L. Morton writes that "the years from 1871 to 1885 were the years in which the position of the Indian in Canada declined from that of an equal to that of a subordinate."[38] This was the direct result of government policy and though the NWMP did not make the policy, they were the main instrument in the North West to carry it out. The police were responsible for moving the Indians to reserves and for keeping them there, and were intimately involved in administering treaties and Indian affairs generally. The myth that the NWMP worked always to defend Indian interests is as false as the contention that the Royal Irish Constabulary existed soley to safeguard the well-being of the Irish. That certain individuals in the Force sympathized with the plight of the Indians and attempted to carry out a disagreeable task in as humane a manner as possible does not alter the nature of the Force and their work. Most police officials knew whose interests they served and knew that to be "too soft on Indians" endangered their career in the Force. J. M. Walsh was transferred from the Wood Mountain detachment in 1880 because he was suspected of being too friendly to Sitting Bull, the famous Sioux chief who found temporary refuge in Canada after the Battle of the Little Big Horn.[39] Prime Minister Macdonald, Commissioner Irvine and Lieutenant-Governor Dewdney suspected Walsh of having encouraged Sitting Bull to remain in Canada, and so they kept Walsh in the East until the starved-out Sitting Bull and his Sioux had returned to the United States.

Even of those police officers who sympathized with the Indians, few questioned the dominant white picture of the NWMP as a "civilizing force" one of whose main tasks was to "tame wild Indian tribes." Their sympathy was generally of the paternalistic "white man's burden" variety. There were also a fair number of out-and-out racists among the police who subscribed to the infamous slogan of many American settlers and soldiers that "the only good Indian is a dead Indian," though there were no instances in Canada of the type of bloodthirsty massacres carried out by the American army against Indians in the United States.

The reminiscences and autobiographies of NWMP officers reveal a variety of attitudes, ranging from considerable respect for and understanding of Indian customs to outright racism. An example of the latter is found in *Sergeant 331*, the personal recollections of F. J. E. Fitzpatrick, who served in the Mounted Police from 1879 to 1885. In describing a sun dance by Cree Indians, Fitzpatrick reveals his racist conceptions of their customs:

> While all this performance was proceeding, each one of the old men of the tribe would in turn assume the post of orator,

and recite for the edification of the younger element the noble and worthy deeds of his life. He told how many horses he had stolen from enemy tribes, and in doing so how cleverly he had used his tomahawk — perhaps on an old woman, who had interfered with his plans; also how many of the captured wounded enemy he had scalped or tortured, going through the most fiendish details.

Herein lies the well-grounded objection by any civilized government to this ceremonial. The deeds recited by the old Indians, and gloried in by them, were all against the laws of God and man, but were put before the eyes and ears of children as proper examples to follow; and it is likely that the latter in turn would not fail to emulate their forefathers.[40]

It is difficult to obtain reliable documentary evidence of the Indian view of the Mounted Police, because the Indians seldom committed anything to paper. What information there is exists mainly in reports, and naturally the police would tend to exaggerate Indian affection or respect for them and de-emphasize negative opinions, especially in subsequent historical accounts. The Indians do appear to have been grateful to the NWMP for suppressing the worst aspects of the whiskey trade and for helping to prevent a recurrence of outrages like the Cypress Hills Massacre. However, the fact that the Force represented the interests who were rapidly destroying the Indian economy and way of life and was frequently called upon to protect those same interests led to a state of constant tension between the police and the Indian nations.

The relationship between the police and the Indians also varied a great deal according to tribe. As we have pointed out, one of the reasons the government hurried up their plans to despatch the Mounted Police to the North West in the first place was to impress the Blackfoot nation. Later there may well have been a conscious attempt by government officials to maintain an unofficial alliance or understanding with the Blackfeet by taking advantage of the fact that they were traditional enemies of the Crees. The strategy of "divide and rule" was certainly not new in North America. If this strategy was consciously employed by the government, it paid off, because the Blackfeet refused offers of an alliance against the whites and declined to participate with the Crees and Metis in the rebellion of 1885. Blackfoot chiefs thereafter became a standard part of the mythical popularity of the police among the Indians. Lieutenant-Governor Dewdney made a special trip to confer with Blackfoot chiefs during the rebellion of 1885, and the government hastened to supply them with more generous provisions for fear they would join the rebellion. Dewdney later suggested using the Blackfeet against the Crees, but the government agent rejected the suggestion on the spot. C. E. Denny, a member of the Force as well as temporary Indian agent during the period of the rebellion, has recorded a telegram, wired in cipher, which he received from Dewdney on May 1, 1885:

> A few Crees around thirty in number around Cypress skulking. Would like Blackfeet to clean them out. Could this be done quietly? Advise me before taking action.[41]

Denny declined to encourage such action by the Blackfeet on the grounds that once it started he might not be able to control it.

During and after the Sackatchewan Rebellion of 1885, any warm feeling that may have existed between the NWMP and the Metis and most of the Indian population ceased. The police were not the cause of the rebellion and, in fact, repeatedly warned the government that unrest and well-founded grievances might lead to open rebellion if concessions were not forthcoming. When the government did not respond and rebellion broke out, the Mounted Police participated along with regular military forces in suppressing it. They were also instrumental in apprehending and meting out punishment to the rebels. Magistrates sentenced 18 Metis and about 30 Indians, including Big Bear and Poundmaker, to penitentiary terms; and they executed Louis Riel and eight Indians: Ikta, Little Bear, Wandering Spirit, Round-the-Sky, Miserable Man, Bad Arrow, Man-Without-Blood and Iron Body. The Indians they executed publicly in the Mounted Police stockade at Battleford. The government "encouraged" Indians from nearby reserves to witness the execution "as it was held that such a tragic spectacle would be an emphatic deterrent against a repetition of such offences."[42] The description of the execution in Turner's official history of the North West Mounted Police indicates clearly the police concept of justice:

> The scaffold, which stood in the open square within the Mounted Police stockade, consisted of a platform about ten

feet high and twenty feet long supported by posts at the corners and two higher posts on either side of the centre with a stout crossbeam between. Beneath this was the trap, surrounded by a railing. Two full divisions of the Mounted Police, "D" and "K", and "A" Battery the regulars from Eastern Canada — about 350 men in all — formed a hollow square surrounding the scaffold. At a respectable distance, the assembled crowd had a complete and uninterrupted view.

As the hour drew near, weird chanting arose from the direction of the Indian camp, and as one by one the condemned were conducted from the barracks the impressive dirge grew louder. Among those about to die there was little evidence of mental agitation; several joked openly or chatted casually. The shackles they had worn were removed, but their arms were pinioned. Each walked between and was preceded and followed by Mounted Police constables. They were soon on the scaffold, each beneath a dangling rope. But before the eight ropes were adjusted and black caps drawn over eight shaven heads, all were told they could speak for ten minutes. Only Ikta and Little Bear availed themselves of the privilege, both shouting defiance. Others uttered a few high pitched war cries or sang their weird lamentations. Wandering Spirit was completely resigned and undemonstrative. Then Hodson spoke, silence fell and the bolt was drawn.

All died instantly. The bodies were hurried away in rough pine boxes and committed to a common grave on the hillside below the barracks.

The days of the scalping knife and war clubs were definitely of the past.[43]

The authorities punished Metis and Indians suspected of having supported the rebellion regardless of whether they had been tried for specific offences. They virtually wiped out the Metis as a distinct national and political group. They burned and looted their homes and destroyed their property. They withheld annuities from those Indian bands that had participated in the rebellion and confiscated their horses and arms. From that time on they made greater efforts to restrict Indians to the reserves and strictly regulated the sale of ammunition to them. Most of these punitive measures were carried out by the Mounted Police. The authorized strength of the Force was increased from 500 to 1,000 men in view of their increased activity and the fact that, since the Indians were now powerless, more settlers would migrate to the North West Territories.

Credit usually goes to the Mounted Police for the fact that the conquest of the Canadian West was not nearly so bloody an affair as that of the Western United States. In fairness they do deserve some credit. The Force was reasonably proficient at controlling outlaws, and the fact that they were well established before large-scale settlement occurred probably discouraged all parties from headlong rushes into the sort of bloodshed that stained the American West. Many of the wars of extermination in the United States began when greedy settlers and merchants called on the army for assistance in what amounted to the mass murder of Indians. The Mounted Police were a small force, which, prior to the completion of the CPR, could not depend upon readily available military assistance. This compelled them to tread lightly when dealing with Indians and to depend more upon skillful diplomacy and less upon brute force than did the American Army. The Indians of Western Canada may also have been more careful to avoid warfare with the white men. They had seen their brothers in the United States mercilessly annihilated by a foe superior in technology and numbers.

The North West Mounted Police between 1873 and 1885 were less brutal than the American Army and from necessity may even have been more humane than most other imperialist forces of that era. Nonetheless they were a crucial part of a conscious scheme by which powerful economic and political interests destroyed the economy and way of life of entire peoples and wrested a vast territory from its inhabitants for a pittance. Anyone who describes the role of the NWMP during this period as constituting the "glorious foundations of a great tradition" must surely be either hopelessly naive or lacking in moral sensitivity.

Chapter 2
The NWMP and the CPR

Originally the North West Mounted Police worked mainly to assert the authority of the federal government over the native inhabitants of the North West. However, they were soon defending the interests of the corporate friends of the government as well, particularly the CPR, against Indians, settlers and their own employees. In this latter capacity members of the Force developed an intimate relationship with the CPR management which continued for decades. The relationship became so close that officers of the Force began to look upon the corporation as almost equivalent to the government and to regard its interests as identical to those of the community as a whole. The railway, after all, supposedly represented advancing civilization. In any dispute between the CPR and the Indians or the CPR and its own employees, the police automatically sided with the corporation and often made no attempt to hide the fact.

On the contrary, they and their apologists boasted about police efforts on behalf of the railway as evidence of the value of the Force, and depicted critics of the CPR either as ignorant savages standing in the way of inevitable progress or as worthless malcontents. R. G. Macbeth expressed these sentiments most forcefully in his historical account of the Force:

It is quite certain that the presence of the men in scarlet and gold on the Western plains was an element in the situation which encouraged the promoters of the Canadian Pacific Railway, our first transcontinental, to undertake their tremendous project with more assured confidence. For these shrewd students of human nature knew quite well that people would look in various ways upon the coming of the railway.

There would be some who, like Thoreau, the hermit sage of Walden, would resist, though perhaps for a less aesthetic reason, the intrusion of the noisy and energetic sign of a new era. It was he who cried, "We do not ride on the railway; it rides on us." For, while there were some in our west who actually did feel regret at the passing of the quiet day of their pioneer life, most of those who had the aggressive spirit of the white race in them, were glad to see the vision of the earliest colonist being fulfilled by the opening up of the country. But there were others who had lived on the frontiers, and had been a law unto themselves, who said, like a trader who saw three wooden shacks built where Calgary now stands, "I am going to move back — this is getting too civilized for me", and the man who said that represented a class that had to be made to realize the presence of the government.

Then there were the Indians, who saw in the advent of the railway the necessary disappearance of big game from the plains, which would become the habitat of the settler. More than once there were Indians who would have blocked the way of the railway builders or would even have swooped down in the night and torn up the rails, but for the restraining presence of authority. And besides all these, there were some amongst the huge gangs of natives and general trackmakers who had alien tastes and habits . . . . [1]

Were critics of the railway unjust to feel that the CPR "rides on us"? Didn't tremendous concessions the government made to the CPR help to ensure that it would quickly become the most powerful corporation in the country? The concessions included:

(1) $25 million in public funds
(2) 25 million acres of the best land in the North West
(3) 700 miles of railway already constructed at government expense
(4) exemption from taxation of all property and capital stock
(5) exemption from import duties of most material used in construction
(6) a monopoly of traffic in certain areas for 20 years.

And they were only the beginning. For many years the government continued to make grants and loans and extend privileges to the CPR. The CPR in turn could use their land grants to get into land colonization companies and the exploitation of timber and mineral resources.

Critics came down heavily on the CPR from the beginning. Many taxpayers objected to the massive government giveaways. Indians in the North West naturally regarded the railway as a threat to their economy, in that it destroyed the wild game and encouraged rapid white settlement. The railway was also the cause of many prairie fires, for which it assumed no responsibility. White settlers too were soon at loggerheads with the CPR over exorbitant freight rates, inadequate service and land speculation. Vast CPR holdings would sit tax-free in an unimproved state until settlers in a particular area had built up their community and thus made the adjacent CPR land valuable. The CPR would then sell the land at a goodly profit that came out of the sweat of the farmers. The white settlers who supported the agitation led by Riel prior to the Saskatchewan Rebellion did so in part to protest the injustices arising from the monopoly position of the CPR and demanded a railway to Hudson Bay as an alternative. The other group frequently fighting the railway was its own work force. Low wages and harsh working and living conditions resulted in much labour unrest and frequent strikes, first among construction workers and later among operating and maintenance employees.

The first task of the NWMP in defence of the CPR was to force the Indians of the North West to accept the intrusion of the railway into their territory. Schoolchildren learn to admire the courage of two Mounted Police officers in moving Chief Piapot and his band from the CPR right-of-way during construction of the railway, just as they learn to recognize in Piapot one of those "worthless malcontents" standing in the way of "law and order." Piapot's "crime" consisted in his assumption that if the CPR was going to construct a railway through his country, they should ask his permission and perhaps provide him and his band with some form of compensation. The CPR soon put a stop to such presumption by appealing to Lieutenant-Governor Dewdney, who turned the matter over to the NWMP. That Piapot did not resist the police by resorting to violence is usually explained by the great respect held by the Indians for the Force. The obvious explanation, of course, is that Piapot *could* not risk violent resistance because he knew that it could bring retribution upon himself and his people at the hands of a powerful military force.

The episode with Piapot was just one of many occasions when the Mounted Police were called upon to protect the CPR from Indian resistance. The rapid construction of the railway in the early 1880s was the main reason for the strength of the Force being increased from 300 to 500 men in 1882 and the headquarters being moved from Fort Walsh to Regina. From 1882 until the completion of the CPR, the Mounted Police devoted a considerable part of their time to patrolling railway property against possible interference from Indians. The CPR certainly gave the Indians plenty of reasons for interference. In 1883, for instance, construction gangs began laying tracks across the main Blackfoot reservation. The land in question had been reserved for the Blackfeet by Indian Treaty No.7, but neither the government nor the CPR had offered compensation or even requested permission to build the railway through the reserve. Not surprisingly the Blackfeet were incensed at this arrogant violation of the treaty and retaliated by tearing up the rails. Many of the Blackfeet were for attacking the construction camps and even going to war, if necessary, to maintain the territorial integrity of their reserve. On this occasion the police were less instrumental in settling the trouble than was Father Albert Lacombe, an influential Oblate missionary, who, along with Chief Crowfoot, persuaded the Blackfeet to allow the CPR to pass through the reserve after assuring them that the government would grant them additional land as compensation. For their efforts Lacombe and Crowfoot received free passes for life on the CPR. Clearly chiefs like Crowfoot made life easier for the white power structure than more militant chiefs like Big Bear and Poundmaker.

The North West Mounted Police began breaking strikes for the CPR during the 1880s. (Eventually strike breaking became a traditional activity of the Force, and by the 1920s and 1930s the Mounties were the most notorious strikebreakers in Canada.) The Force was called upon to smash two strikes during 1883. The first was a strike of about 130 construction workers near Maple Creek during the summer. About 30 police officers under Inspector Sam. B. Steele broke it. They arrested and imprisoned the leaders, allegedly for assaulting a foreman, "while other prompt steps were taken to suppress revolt by his followers."[2] In December of the same year, the CPR reduced the wages of its engineers during an economy drive occasioned by the financial difficulties of the company.[3] The engineers struck for restoration of the previous wage rate. The CPR then locked some of its other employees out of the shops and roundhouses and refused to allow them to return to work unless they agreed not to support the engineers.[4] The company also recruited scab engineers and threatened to fire any strikers who did not return to work on company terms.[5] The CPR then called upon the assistance of the NWMP on the alleged grounds that the strikers had damaged company property and sabotaged engines. The engineers, it should be noted, denied responsibility for any such damages.

The NWMP came to the assistance of the CPR, but they did not confine themselves to preventing damage and sabotage. They were used in large numbers to intimidate the strikers and in some cases as scabs to actually run the trains. An article on the strike in the *Manitoba Daily Free Press* of December 17, 1883 datelined Regina, December16, stated, "An engine and two cars arrived yesterday afternoon from Moose Jaw returning the same day with thirty-five Mounted Police and two officers." The same article mentioned that the Mounted Police had assumed charge of the Medicine Hat roundhouse, and that Colonel Herchmer and 16 Mounties were on another train. The incident involving the 35 Mounties who proceeded from Regina to Moose Jaw was later described by F. J. E. Fitzpatrick, one of the officers in charge, in *Sergeant 331*.[6] According to Fitzpatrick, the CPR superintendent in Moose Jaw, having made arrangements with NWMP headquarters in advance, managed to "steal away" from Moose Jaw with a locomotive and a car and picked up the 35 men under Fitzpatrick's command. Fitzpatrick describes the arrival of his contingent of armed men in Moose Jaw:

> Upon arriving at the station, we found about 400 men, who were intent on stopping what they thought was a mail train. Their astonishment was unbounded when they saw our men emerge with revolvers and Winchesters, ready for business. I issued an order, which I signed, and which the superintendent of the Canadian Pacific Railway division had countersigned, to the effect that no one would be allowed on the grounds of the Canadian Pacific Railway. My men, therefore, proceeded to clear the premises with loaded carbines in hand.[7]

The striking engineers and locked-out employees had to return to work within a few weeks largely on company terms. That the NWMP were instrumental in ensuring a victory for the CPR is evident not only from their acts of intimidation against the strikers and their supporters but also from the fact that they filled in where there was a shortage of scabs. Fitzpatrick describes this with considerable pride:

> Our men took charge to some of the mail trains and ran them from Winnipeg clear to the Rockies. It was strange, but our force seemed to possess men who could do almost anything when the occasion demanded it.[8]

The *Regina Leader* of December 27, 1883, reported, "On Monday a train arrived in Brandon, the engine driven by Mr. Walter R. Johnston of the North West Mounted Police and Mr. Thomas Hewitt of Regina, and formerly engineer of the *Leader* office." The same edition of the *Regina Leader* carried an editorial denouncing the engineers for having refused to sign a CPR contract stating they were "satisfied" with the reduced wage rates, and congratulating Superintendent Egan of the CPR for demanding that the men sign such a contract or be fired. The NWMP were obviously not the only ones proud to be associated with scabbing for the railway.

The NWMP saw their role in the strike as a matter of self-congratulation and boasted considerably about it in the annual report of the Force for 1883. Colonel Herchmer, who was in charge of controlling strikers at Broadview, reported:

> On arrival there, I took charge of all the railway property. There was a good deal of excitement among the strikers, and I have no hesitation in saying that if it had not been for our men there would have been serious trouble . . . Besides guarding the roundhouse, every engine which left the yard was guarded.[9]

Commissioner Irvine thought the Force deserved the whole credit for smashing the strike: "I shall only add that the prompt and I trust effectual, quelling of what at one time appeared to be a universal railway strike is . . . a matter of the utmost congratulation."[10]

The fact that the leading officers of the Mounted Police boasted proudly of their role in the strike reflects not only their anti-labour bias but also their desire to carry favour with the CPR, the government and the press. To be in good standing with such powerful groups would more than offset the public criticism, discussed in the previous chapter, to which the Force was increasingly subjected. Bouquets were soon forthcoming from the CPR. Superintendent Egan, in a letter highly appreciative of the services rendered by the Force during 1883, mentioned the strike as an example: "The services of your men during recent trouble among a certain class of our employees, prevented destruction to property, and preserved obedience to law and order in a manner highly commendable."[11] The press, which had sometimes been critical of the police, was also pleased at their efficiency in helping to smash the strike. An editorial in the *Regina Leader* of January 3, 1884, declared, "The Mounted Police have progressed in efficiency, and on several occasions . . . especially in connection with the late railway strike . . . have shown how admirably adapted they are to meet the needs of a country in the position of the North-West."[12] They were certainly meeting the needs of someone.

As CPR construction proceeded into British Columbia, the NWMP were given jurisdiction over a twenty-mile belt, with the railroad in the middle of it, which the federal government had declared to be under the Act for the Preservation of Peace on Public Works. This act dated back to the 1850s when police and troops were frequently used to smash strikes during the construction of railways and canals in Ontario and Quebec. The Mounted Police were soon as busy breaking strikes and intimidating workers as they had been on the prairies.

On April 1, 1885, several hundred construction workers who had not been paid for three months struck in protest at a place called the Beaver in the Rocky Mountains. The pro-Mounted Police accounts of this episode describe it as an heroic event in the history of the Force on the grounds that a small contingent of police officers were able to disperse a large demonstration which they themselves had provoked. Colonel Sam Steele, then a Mounted Police superintendent in charge of the detachment at the Beaver, has described the role of the Force in the strike in *Forty Years in Canada*.[13] In telling the story from the viewpoint of the Force and the CPR, Steele reveals that he and his detachment were by no means neutral: "I assured them that they made a great mistake in striking and that, if they committed any act of violence and were not orderly in the strictest sense of the word, I should inflict on the offenders the severest punishment the law would allow me."[14]

Steele's police were soon busy maintaining "law and order." Some strikers returned to work after assurances by the construction manager that their pay would soon be arriving. Several hundred continued the strike and attempted to prevent the resumption of work. However, track laying continued in a narrow canyon while the police mounted guard at the entrance to keep the strikers at bay. The Mounties later arrested one of the strike leaders and alleged that he was inciting strikers to attack the police barracks. This provoked what turned into a virtual riot when a crowd attempted to free the prisoner. The crowd dispersed after being read the Riot Act accompanied by a show of force by the Mounties and others described by Steele as "a considerable number of engineers, respectable merchants and contractors, all well armed . . . ." The next day the Mounties arrested several more people as the alleged "ringleaders" in the attempt to free the prisoner.

On this occasion Steele deemed it unwise to inflict the severest punishment allowed by law, probably because the Saskatchewan Rebellion had just broken out and he knew that he could not hope for reinforcements. Instead he sentenced the arrested men to a $100 fine or six months' imprisonment in the hope that such punishments would suffice to deter further outbreaks.

> We were right; no further trouble occurred. The strike had collapsed, the roughs of the Beaver, having had a lesson were quiet. I was much pleased and so were all the contractors, Mr. Ross especially.[15]

Mr. Ross was James Ross, the engineer in charge of CPR railway construction. Later Superintendent Steele was recognized for his services by being invited to accompany CPR and government dignitaries on the first passenger train ride to the Pacific.

The CPR management had cause to be pleased with the Mounties during and after the Saskatchewan Rebellion. The directors not only had a vested interest in crushing the rebellion but also took advantage of it to demonstrate the usefulness of the railway to the government and the British financial community. The CPR was then engaged in attempting to sell bonds in England and to persuade the Canadian government to supply more handouts. Neither enterprise looked very hopeful until the rebellion broke out, when Van Horne, seeing an opportunity to promote the railway, quickly offered to transport troops free of charge if necessary and to give the government priority in the use of railway facilities and equipment. Much was made of the fact that without the CPR, troops from central Canada would have required several weeks to reach the North West. The whole affair paid off for the CPR. In July 1885, Parliament voted an additional $5 million grant to the railway. The quick suppression of the rebellion also increased the prospects for rapid settlement and helped the CPR to sell $15 million worth of bonds on the London market.

The 1880s saw the beginning of a long period of collaboration among the CPR, the government, the Mounted Police and the military. Together they were instrumental in smashing strikes and curbing trade union activities for half a century. They did not, however, confine themselves to Canada but were instrumental in suppressing challenges to British imperialism in other parts of the world as well. During the Boer War, for example, Donald A. Smith, the railway magnate who drove "the last spike" in 1885 and became Lord Strathcona and Mount Royal raised and equipped at his own expense a regiment known as Strathcona's Horse to fight for the British in South Africa. The regiment was commanded by none other than Sam Steele of the NWMP, and many of the officers and men were also from the Force. Mounted Police Commissioner L. W. Herchmer was given command of another regiment in the war, also consisting of many members of the Force.

Donald Smith was a robber baron of the first order. He bagan his career as a Hudson's Bay Company agent in 1838 and proceeded to make a fortune by, among other things, exploiting the Indians of Labrador to the point of starvation.[16] One of the richest and most powerful men in Canada, he became governor of the Hudson's Bay Company, chief shareholder and president of the Bank of Montreal and one of the largest shareholders of the CPR. Smith was also an M.P. for many years and once had to resign his seat because of corrupt practices. He was eventually made a baron and Canadian High Commissioner to London. Smith and his collaborators in the business and political world became virtual patrons of the NWMP and were on a first-name basis with many of the leading personalities of the Force. With such friends, it is little wonder that the top officials in the Mounted Police instilled an anti-labour bias in the Force.

Chapter 3
War, workers and strikes

In 1904 the name North West Mounted Police was changed to Royal North West Mounted Police in recognition of service to the Empire. In the next few years the Force underwent a period of expansion. The West was settled very rapidly in the period from 1900 to 1914. In 1905 Saskatchewan and Alberta achieved provincial status. When these new provinces retained the RNWMP to act in the capacity of provincial police rather than establishing new forces of their own, it looked as though the future of the Force was assured in the West. The Eastern provinces had provincial police forces and the Dominion Police. The Dominion Police had some jurisdiction throughout Canada though it was concentrated in the East. They specialized in enforcing federal acts and also operated as political police to keep an eye on "subversives" and other enemies of the prevailing system.

For the first couple of years of World War I, both the Dominion Police and the RNWMP were kept extra busy. Social unrest, which had been growing as the country industrialized before 1914, increased with the strains brought on by the war. From the beginning there had been only lukewarm support for the war in Quebec and among certain sections of the labour and agrarian movements in English Canada. This significant minority increased in numbers and was further alienated by the way the war was conducted at home and abroad. On the home front profiteering, gross corruption, outrageous price increases and deteriorating working and living conditions became a national scandal. On the fighting front incompetent leadership and heavy casualties, sometimes caused, as in the case of the Ross rifle, by shoddy equipment supplied by friends of the government, caused much bitterness. The government did very little to curb profiteering and corruption, but a great deal to suppress critics of the war effort by using the War Measures Act to deny them their civil rights. Critics of the war and the way it was conducted included most Quebecois and large numbers of reformers, socialists and pacifists in the trade union and farm movements across the country. The government attempted to silence such critics by means of strict censorship, internment, police harassment and propaganda branding critics of the war effort as unpatriotic and pro-German.

The real crunch came with the imposition of military conscription under the Military Service Act in 1917. Conscription was anathema in Quebec and was opposed by a large and militant minority elsewhere. The federal government relied upon troops to maintain control in Quebec when the enforcement of conscription was met with demonstrations, riots and street fights. The government took dictatorial measures to combat draft evasion and criticism of conscription throughout Canada. Section 16 of the Military Service Act empowered the government, with the approval of the central appeal judge, to suppress any publication containing matters thought to hinder the operation of the act.[1] This, along with regulations under the War Measures Act, made it extremely risky for anyone offering militant opposition to conscription. That the authorities were prepared to use their increased power is indicated by the thousands of arrests. During 1917 and the first three months of 1918, 3,895 people were arrested on charges connected with anti-conscriptionist activity.[2] Some received fairly lengthy prison sentences. A few were less fortunate and were seriously injured or killed while evading the draft or participating in anti-conscription demonstrations. One case of what passed for "justice" involved Albert (Ginger) Goodwin, a past president of the British Columbia Federation of Labour and an organizer for the Mine, Mill and Smelter Workers in 1918.[3] Goodwin had been called before a conscription board in 1917 and placed in class D, that is, unfit for military service because of his health. Later, while Goodwin was leading a strike of smeltermen in Trail, he was by a strange coincidence ordered to report for immediate active service. Like hundreds of other opponents of the war, Goodwin went into hiding in the wilderness. On July 26, 1918, Goodwin was shot dead in the bush by officers of the Dominion Police who were searching for draft dodgers. This outrage provoked a one-day general strike throughout much of British Columbia. During the strike soldiers organized by city businessmen ransacked the Vancouver Labour Temple and badly beat at least two labour leaders.[4]

It fell to the RNWMP during the early part of the war to

assist the Dominion Police and other forces in maintaining internal order and harassing opponents of the war effort. The RNWMP were still mainly in the Western provinces, though occasionally they loaned personnel to the Dominion Police for use in other parts of Canada. In the Western provinces they carried out investigations in districts where there were large numbers of "enemy aliens" and patrolled the international boundary with the United States. The United States was a neutral country until 1917 and the authorities feared, apparently quite unnecessarily, that German-Americans might make raids into Canada for the purpose of sabotage. The term "enemy alien" was used to refer to residents of Canada who had emigrated from countries controlled by Germany and Austria-Hungary. This included a large part of central and south-eastern Europe and, after the Bolshevik Revolution of 1917, the term was broadened to include as well all immigrants from countries and territories that had belonged to Czarist Russia and were to become part of the Soviet Union. The so-called "enemy aliens" numbered in excess of 200,000 in the Prairie provinces alone. They suffered considerable harassment during the war by the authorities and the super-patriots among the public. Hundreds were interned on the grounds that they endangered or might endanger the war effort. Besides watching "enemy aliens", the RNWMP kept an eye on socialists, pacifists and trade union activists who were actively opposed to the war. The police also assisted the authorities in enforcing regulations under the War Measures Act. It was during this period that Commissioner A. B. Perry constructed a network of plainclothes detectives and undercover men who were to comprise part of the Security and Intelligence branch (S and I), which was to become notorious in later years as Canada's secret police.

By 1917 the number of RNWMP on active duty in Canada had begun to dwindle significantly. Saskatchewan and Alberta established provincial police forces of their own and, with the United States' entry into the war, the obvious fact that the "enemy aliens" were causing no trouble, and the demand for reinforcements on the battlefield, the Force decided to allow many of its members to join the regular army. A special squadron of RNWMP was also formed in 1918 and sent to Siberia to fight for the reactionary forces in the Russian civil war. The Annual Report of the RNWMP for the year ending September 30, 1918, noted that there were then 52 officers and 1,169

N.C.O.'s and constables officially in the Force and an additional 12 officers and 726 others on leave overseas.[5] Shortly after September 30, another 174 were despatched to Siberia leaving only slightly more than 300, or about the same number the Force started out with in 1874, on active duty in Canada. The report also noted that the Mounted Police had been assisting in the enforcement of the Military Service Act and that some of their personnel had been loaned to the Dominion Police, including 20 who had been sent to Quebec under Superintendent Starnes. During 1916 and 1917 there had been considerable talk of disbanding the RNWMP after the war and leaving policing entirely to the provinces and the Dominion Police. Many people failed to see the need for a semi-military mounted police force under federal auspices now that frontier conditions no longer existed and the whole country except for the sparsely settled North West Territories and Yukon had achieved provincial status. What saved the RNWMP from abolition as a force was intense industrial and social unrest at the end of World War I. Events during this period caused great anxiety in business and governmental circles, and the Mounted Police assured their own future by making themselves invaluable to the economic and political elite of the day.

The industrial unrest which had been increasing since 1914 reached unprecedented proportions by 1917. Rapid urbanization brought on by the quick growth of war industries caused a deterioration in working and living conditions. Inflationary price increases were an added burden on the poor. By 1917 there were more trade unionists than ever before and more people went on strike than in any previous year in Canadian history. The military conscription of manpower and more stringent enforcement of the War Measures Act added to the frustration of the trade union radicals. There were prolonged and militant strikes in 1918, including one which nearly developed into a general strike in Winnipeg. Unrest was especially widespread in Western Canada, where many trade unionists were not only critical of the economic system but also alienated from the more conservative Eastern leadership of the Trades and Labour Congress (TLC).

The federal government reacted to an unstable situation by imposing ever harsher measures, to the point where they increased the probability of a major explosion at the end of the war. The government stepped up secret police activities and appointed C. H. Cahan, a prominent corporation lawyer, to survey conditions throughout the country and recommend a course of action.[6] The police found no evidence of a revolutionary conspiracy afoot, and Cahan reported that the unrest was due primarily not to radical agitators but to general disillusionment with the war, disgust at the performance of the federal government and deteriorating economic conditions:

> I am convinced that the unrest now prevalent in Canada is due to the weakening of the moral purpose of the people to prosecute the war to a successful end; to the fact that people are becoming daily more conscious of the bloody sacrifices and irritating burdens entailed by carrying on the war; and to the growing belief that the Union government is failing to deal effectively with the financial, industrial and economic problems growing out of the war *which are, perhaps, incapable of any early satisfactory solution.*[7] [Italics added]

The problems growing out of the war became more immediate after the armistice. The closing down of armament and munitions factories and the disbanding of a large army caused widespread unemployment and a generally depressed economy. Added to this was the fact that workers who had made sacrifices during the war now demanded the gains which had been postponed in the name of the war effort. Soldiers returning from the front also demanded jobs and the chance for a decent life after fighting "the war to make the world safe for democracy." Most of these people were to be sadly disappointed, and their disappointment was not long in turning to frustration and anger.

Unrest increased as the government failed to tackle the problems which Cahan had described as "incapable of an early satisfactory solution." To really tackle such problems would mean demanding concessions from the vested interests which had fattened on the war effort, and the government was not about to attempt such a solution. Since Cahan recognized this clearly, he recommended instead repressive measures designed to maintain order over a difficult period of post-war readjustment. The government established a Department of Public Safety with Cahan as director. Numerous Orders-in-Council were passed under the War Measures Act to provide for the following: (1) broadening the category described as "enemy alien" and requiring the registration of all such people, (2) severely restricting the right to strike, (3) prohibiting publications in 14 languages, (4) prohibiting the use of several foreign languages at public meetings, (5) declaring 14 different organizations to be illegal, including such moderate groups as the Social Democratic Party, and (6) allowing the authorities to declare any association unlawful.[8] To implement these sweeping measures required greatly increased police activity, and during the last months of 1918 and early 1919 the federal government began to build up the strength of the RNWMP and assign to them many duties previously undertaken by the Dominion Police.

By the time a major showdown between capital and labour came in the form of the Winnipeg General Strike in May, 1919, the government and business community in Canada had become extremely frightened by growing labour radicalism. Western labour radicals had been busy laying plans for the organization of the One Big Union (OBU) a large industrial union which they hoped would eventually embrace all workers and struggle for the overthrow of the capitalist system as well as fight for immediate economic gains. The British Columbia Federation of Labour and many trade union councils and locals throughout the West endorsed the OBU idea and called for major economic concessions, removal of restrictions on civil liberties and the release of political prisoners. The Western Labour militants held a conference in Calgary in March, 1919, known as the Western Labour Conference, and laid plans to hold a referendum in union locals throughout the West on the question of severing relations with international craft unions and forming the One Big Union. They agreed that if the results were encouraging, they would hold a conference later in the year for the founding of the OBU. They also expressed sympathy with the Bolshevik Revolution and threatened a general strike by June 1 if Canadian forces were not withdrawn from Russia. All of these activities in Canada coupled with the recent revolution in Russia and revolutionary developments in other parts of Europe helped to create an uneasiness among Canada's ruling elite which bordered on hysteria and grossly exaggerated the possibility of an attempted revolution in this country.

Before the referendum on the OBU could be completed or any effective organization established the Winnipeg General Strike, under more moderate leadership than the OBU and with very limited aims, broke out on May 15.[9] The events leading to the general strike began on May 1, when the workers in the building and metal trades struck on the issues of higher wages and the right to collective bargaining. The employers not only refused the wage demands but also refused to recognize the Metal Trades Council as the common bargaining agent of the unions. The unions took their case to the Winnipeg Trades and Labour Council, which conducted a referendum among its affiliates on the question of a general strike on the issues of collective bargaining and the need for general wage increases. The result was overwhelmingly in favour, and on May 15, 30,000 workers left their jobs, 12,000 of whom were not members of trade unions but who joined the strike spontaneously. The population of Winnipeg in 1919 was about 180,000; 30,000 strikers and their families therefore probably represented at least half of the population. The strikers included municipal, public utility and post office employees. Even the city police voted to strike.

The general strike paralyzed the entire city and the strikers found it necessary to direct their operations by means of a strike committee and a disciplined organization if they were to prevent general disorder and avoid unnecessary hardships to the population as a whole. The city police returned to work at the request of the Strike Committee in order to prevent looting and outbursts of vandalism and violence. Milk and bread deliveries were resumed and essential services like the city water works resumed limited operations by permission of the Strike Committee. The strike was conducted in an exceptionally peaceful manner, and this helped to gain wide public support in Winnipeg and other cities where there were several sympathetic strikes and talk of general walkouts. Indeed several of the strike leaders were pacifists who abhorred violence, and the rank-and-file were repeatedly warned to remain peaceful and beware of provocateurs who might attempt to provoke violent incidents as a means of discrediting the entire strike. For a time it appeared probable that the employers would have to yield to the workers' demands.

However, the forces of capital and the State soon united in a powerful combination to smash the general strike at all costs. All three levels of government, the business and professional communities and the press began a campaign designed to create an atmosphere of hysteria throughout the country by depicting the strike as the beginning of a bloody revolution engineered by the Bolsheviks and supporters of the OBU. A Citizens' Committee of 1,000 organized by professional and businessmen in Winnipeg to break the strike worked closely with government agencies, including the RNWMP. The Mounted Police did not act simply as the military arm of government but played an active role in the propaganda campaign as well. Commissioner Perry made public speeches denouncing the strike and specialized in fostering anti-labour sentiments among the farming population. On May 21 Perry appeared before the executive of the Saskatchewan Grain Growers' Association (SGGA) to describe the strike as an OBU conspiracy aimed at confiscating all private property and establishing a communist form of government.[10] This type of official lying was soon paying dividends for the employers and the government. Some farm leaders joined the anti-labour crusade and J. B. Musselmann, secretary of the SGGA, made the headlines on several occasions with dire predictions about a "red peril" threatening Canada.

As the propaganda campaign got underway throughout Canada, the attitude of government officials and some employers hardened towards the strikers. Early in the strike federal Minister of Labour Gideon Robertson gave the postal workers an ultimatum of returning to work or losing their jobs. When fewer than one-quarter returned, the government dismissed the rest and proceeded to recruit scabs. The Winnipeg City Council fired the regular police force, which had been doing an excellent job of maintaining order without resorting to violent tactics, after they refused to sign a "yellow dog" contract stipulating that they must not be associated with the trade union movement. The regular police were replaced by "specials" recruited with the help of the Citizens' Committee; some of these specials rode on horses donated by the T. Eaton Company. The council also fired all civic employees who refused to return to work and replaced them with scabs. The provincial government adopted the same policy towards employees of the publicly-owned telephone system.

The federal authorities seemed prepared to take a more militant anti-labour position even than many Winnipeg employers. Minister of Labour Gideon Robertson was opposed in principal to any significant concessions to the strikers: "This is not an opportune time to make a declaration in favour of the principle of collective bargaining as it would be grasped as an excuse by the strikers to claim that they have forced the government and thereby proved the success of sympathetic strike."[11] When it appeared that the metal employers were about to recognize collective bargaining and the strike might be settled on reasonable terms, acting Justice Minister Arthur Meighen cautioned against any settlement which might be interpreted as a victory for the strikers.[12] It was obvious that the federal government was determined to defeat the strike as a lesson to labour across the country that general strikes and similar kinds of militant tactics could not succeed.

The RNWMP fit into the picture as a well-trained military force upon whom the authorities could absolutely rely. The RNWMP could also spy on the activities of the strikers and arrest strike leaders. That many regular soldiers would not do such jobs is obvious from the fact that a clear majority of returned soldiers in Winnipeg were supporters of the strike and were, in fact, more militant than the civilian strikers. When the 27th Battalion arrived back in Winnipeg from overseas during the strike, only two members of the entire battalion volunteered for service in Winnipeg.[13] The authorities thereupon promptly disbanded the batallion, and General Ketchen, the Commanding Officer in Winnipeg, recruited volunteers instead for four militia units, knowing of course, that only men opposed to the strike would volunteer. The authorities also sent additional machine guns to Winnipeg surreptitiously, and made arrangements to demobilize a squadron of RNWMP returning from overseas in Winnipeg and place them at the disposal of Commissioner Perry.[14] If soldiers in the regular army could not always be relied on to break civilian strikes, members of the Mounted Police, with a long tradition of anti-labour activity, could.

The government prepared to bear down on the strikers not only by making military preparations but also by providing themselves with more sweeping legal powers in case they were needed. On June 5 Parliament passed a bill amending the Immigration Act in order to make it possible to deport British subjects not born in Canada. This amendment was aimed at the Winnipeg strike leaders, most of whom were British immigrants albeit long-time residents of Canada. The amendment was passed through the House of Commons in 20 minutes and within the hour had been approved by the Senate and given royal assent.[15] Later Parliament also passed what became known as Section 98 of the Criminal Code. Section 98 made it a crime, punishable by up to 20 years in prison, to belong to any association whose purpose was to bring about governmental, industrial or economic change by force or which advocated or defended the use of force for such purposes. The property belonging to such an association might be seized without warrant and forfeited to the Crown. If it could be shown that a person had attended meetings for such an association, spoken publicly in its support or distributed its literature, "it shall be presumed, in the absence of proof to the contrary, that he is a member of such unlawful association." Persons printing, distributing, selling or importing material advocating or defending the use of force might also be imprisoned for up to 20 years. Section 98 remained on the statute books for 16 years and was an effective instrument for intimidating and sometimes imprisoning radicals. It made people cautious about being associated with any protest group because of the possibility that the organization in question might be declared an "unlawful association." Lest the above-mentioned Acts might not be sufficient, the government also amended Section 134 of the Criminal Code to change the maximum penalty for sedition from 2 to 20 years in prison.

The Mounted Police arrested eight of the most important strike leaders and four less prominent strikers on the night of June 16-17. They were acting under instructions from A. J. Andrews, agent of the federal Department of Justice and prominent leader of the Citizens' Committee. A few days later J. S. Woodsworth, an important supporter of the strikers and temporary editor of *Western Labour News,* was arrested and the paper banned. Still later Fred Dixon, who continued for a few days in hiding to put out the paper, gave himself up to the police. The original intention of the government had been to deport seven of the eight main strike leaders (only one had been born in Canada).[16] This plan was abandoned for fear of the public reaction it would cause and because of strong protests from trade unionists across Canada. Instead strike leaders were released on bail in a few days, to be tried later for seditious conspiracy.

The arrest of the strike leaders was the beginning of a concerted attempt by the RNWMP to crush not only the Winnipeg General Strike but the militant wing of the trade union movement throughout the country by means of arrests, harassment, deportations and brute force. The first fatal casualties of this drive occurred in Winnipeg on June 21. The strike supporters among the returned soldiers organized a silent parade to protest the actions of the authorities. Banned by the mayor, the parade took place anyway, until it was brutally broken up by the RNWMP and the "specials" who had been hired to replace the regular city police. About 50 Mounted Police swinging baseball bats rode through the crowd twice. When two of their riders were unhorsed, they drew their revolvers and fired volleys into the crowd. Mike Sokolowiski, who appears to have been only a spectator, was killed instantly of a bullet through his heart, and Steve Schezerbanower was fatally wounded. Dozens more in the crowd were wounded. Mounties and specials wielding clubs then cleared the streets. Masters describes a fight which took place in Hell's Alley:

> A portion of the crowd, estimated at about two hundred, had taken refuge in the alley which ran between Market and James Streets. Here they were caught by specials who entered from both ends. The specials attacked with batons, and at one stage with revolvers, while the crowd retaliated with bricks and missiles. The struggle lasted only ten minutes, from 3:40 to 3:50, but produced twenty-seven casualties before the crowd was overwhelmed.[17]

After clearing the streets, the military assumed control. Immediately they banned public meetings and demonstrations.

The arrest of the strike leaders and the banning of any effective action successfully broke the back of the strike, which was called off on June 25. The strikers were promised some economic gains, a partial recognition of collective bargaining rights and a Royal Commission to look into the causes of the strike.

Following the strike, the government continued a virtual reign of terror against the OBU throughout Canada. Raids on the offices of the OBU and other militant labour and political groups were frequent, in Winnipeg, Brandon, Fort William, Vancouver, Calgary, Lethbridge, Edmonton, Regina, Toronto, Montreal and Ottawa.[18] Literature and files were seized for use by the prosecution in trying the Winnipeg strike leaders for seditious conspiracy. The authorities were determined to link the leaders of the One Big Union to the Winnipeg General Strike. Thus they would be able to justify their actions during the strike as well as their prolonged attack on the OBU for allegedly conspiring to overthrow constituted authority. In addition to gathering evidence for use against the strike leaders, the raiding parties served to spread fear through the radical community. Raids on private dwellings often occurred at night

and included vandalism and sometimes violence. In Winnipeg,
Rev. William Ivens was arrested in the middle of the night
while his children stood by crying.[19] Alderman John Queen
was arrested at the home of A. A. Heaps, later a Labour M.P.;
police broke down the door, ransacked the place and took the
two men away in handcuffs. No labour militant or political
radical could be sure that he or she was not next on the list.
Grace MacInnis, daughter of J. S. Woodsworth and now a
New Democratic M.P., has described how she was instructed
by her mother, who was teaching at Gibson's Landing, British
Columbia, to bury left wing books in the woods lest they be
seized by police as evidence against her father.

All eight strike leaders were tried for seditious conspiracy in
January, 1920. Crown prosecutors included A. J. Andrews
and at least one other prominent member of the Citizens'
Committee. The jurymen all came from rural Manitoba,
where considerable anti-Labour hysteria had been whipped up,
and there was some evidence of undue Crown influence in
choosing the jury. Some of the testimony was provided by
police spies including Mounted Police Corporal F. W. Zaneth,
who had been infiltrating labour organizations for some time
before the strike. Seven of the eight strike leaders were convicted of seditious conspiracy and sentenced to terms ranging
from six months to two years. After Fred Dixon was tried for
seditious libel and acquitted, the Crown declined to press an
identical charge against J. S. Woodsworth. In addition, a number of immigrants involved in the strike were deported, and
many of the victims of what could only be described as the
police riot of June 21 were fined and others imprisoned for
rioting and unlawful assembly.

Although authorities had won the day in the courts, the
voters soon had the chance to express their opinion of the
strike leaders. They elected William Ivens, John Queen and
George Armstrong to the Manitoba Legislature in 1920. At
the time of the election, Ivens and Armstrong were still in
prison! In the federal election of 1921, the voters also elected
J. S. Woodsworth M.P. for Winnipeg North.

The Manitoba government appointed the Robson Commission to examine the causes and conduct of the Winnipeg
General Strike. The Robson Report indicated that the strike
was neither an OBU conspiracy nor any other kind of conspiracy designed to overthrow constituted authority. The purposes of the strike were exactly what the strike leaders and the

rank-and-file had claimed they were: to achieve economic concessions and to gain recognition of collective bargaining rights. Robson found the causes of the strike to be the high cost of living, profiteering, inadequate wages and poor social conditions in general. Robson's findings were conveniently ignored by the government, most employers and especially the RNWMP. To save face the federal authorities and the police had to perpetuate the belief that the strike had been a seditious conspiracy aimed at overthrowing the economic and political system. Many of them, of course, sincerely believed their own propaganda.

Perhaps no group gained more in the short run by the defeat of the Winnipeg General Strike than the RNWMP. The force people thought might be disbanded a year or two earlier had suddenly earned the undying gratitude of most of the daily press. Nora Kelly, who wrote *The Men of the Mounted* in 1949 and submitted it in advance to RCMP Commissioner S. T. Wood, "who kindly had the manuscript read and so made sure that the information contained therein was correctly presented from the point of view of the Mounted Police," claims that the role of the Force during and after the Winnipeg strike was instrumental in persuading the federal government to create the Royal Canadian Mounted Police in November 1919.[20] Although as Kelly's assessment appears to be accurate in this case, unrest prior to the strike had probably already persuaded the government to continue the RNWMP at least in Western Canada. The authorized strength of the Force was set at 1,200 in December 1918 and then suddenly increased to 2,500 in July 1919.[21] By September 30, 1919, the government had already built the Force up to a strength of 1,600 and in November the act was passed to absorb the Dominion Police into the RNWMP and change the name to Royal Canadian Mounted Police. The new order officially took effect as of February 1, 1920.

The new name indicated that the Force would now exercise authority throughout Canada and not just in the Western provinces. The military structure was maintained intact, with special emphasis on the RCMP as an efficient organization for breaking strikes and dispersing urban crowds. During this same period the government was also beefing up the militia for the purpose of maintaining internal order. In June 1919, the Militia Act was amended to allow for a permanent force of 10,000 men which was double what it had been before 1914.

The minister of militia said the reason for this was to aid the civil power should the need arise. The non-permanent active militia (NPAM) was reactivated about the same time in order "to establish an organization throughout the Dominion to which, should attempts at subversion be made, the patriotic elements of the community could rally. Training in the militia would, without doubt, promote the cause of peace and order and be productive of better citizens." In his comments in the annual RCMP report for 1920, N. W. Rowell, the minister responsible for the RCMP, clearly regarded the Force as an important part of the state military apparatus. Rowell noted that the strength of the RCMP had increased to 74 officers and 1,734 N.C.O.'s and constables by June 1920, but added: "I think that so soon as the Militia is definitely re-organized and put upon a sound basis and the Permanent Force is put in shape, so that we may return to pre-war conditions, the strength of the Mounted Police can be decreased."[22]

That the RCMP was created as both a military and political police force and that its top officers leaned towards the far right in political persuasion is obvious from an examination of Commissioner Perry's Annual Report for the year ending September 30, 1919.[23] The RNWMP had been given a much more explicitly political-military character during the year leading up to the creation of the RCMP on a Canada-wide basis. The report emphasized that aside from enforcing specific federal statutes, guarding public buildings and other duties which are normally assigned to a police force and are not explicitly political in nature, the Mounted Police were to serve in the enforcement of "all Orders-in-Council passed under the 'War Measures Act', for protection of public safety" and "generally to aid and assist the civil powers in the preservation of law and order wherever the Government of Canada may direct." It also noted that the government had taken pains to remove RNWMP squadrons from Europe and Siberia as soon as possible so as to increase the total strength in Canada. Commissioner Perry thought that there were enough reserves on hand to meet any emergencies as well as "to supervise the mining and industrial areas, to watch the settlements of enemy nationality and foreigners whose sentiments might be disloyal and attitudes antagonistic." He pointed out that the Force had taken over the secret service from the Dominion Police during the year and had been busy registering and controlling enemy aliens. Perry lamented the presence of unrest in

Western Canada and observed that "some of the strikes have had a sinister purpose although probably not realized by many who took part." The report pointed out that several people had been convicted for possessing prohibited literature, "but there is a flood of pernicious and mischievous literature not on the prohibited list. Under the cloak of freedom of thought and speech, this literature is being spread for the avowed purpose of overthrowing democratic government and destroying the foundation of civilization." Perry claimed that "seditious societies" were thriving on the unrest, but the members of at least one, the Vancouver branch of the Russian Workers' Union, were under orders for deportation.

Perhaps the most revealing part of the report was the inclusion of a report of Superintendent Starnes, commanding officer of the Manitoba district, to Commissioner Perry on the Winnipeg Strike. Starnes mentioned that the regular city police had to be replaced by volunteers because "it was plainly seen that their sympathy was with the disturbing element." He also boasted that the RNWMP had stood by in readiness and that "our plainclothes men and special agents were constantly keeping in touch with all agitation, and reports on the situation were submitted to you regularly." Starnes explained that the RNWMP force sent to disperse the banned parade of June 21 had consisted of 54 mounted men and 36 men in trucks with an additional reserve kept in the barracks. He went on to portray that capacity for distorting facts which by then had become characteristic of Mounted Police officers:

> On arrival on the main street near the city hall, our men were received with showers of stones, shots and other missiles. A couple of men were dismounted through their horses falling, and were in danger. The mob got so aggressive that the officer commanding the mounted men had to give the order to draw their revolvers and use them. This had the desired effect and the streets were soon cleared and the mob kept in check.
>
> There were 16 of our men wounded with missiles, 4 of whom had to remain in hospital for several days. *During the riot, one foreigner was killed, one fatally wounded and an unknown number wounded.* From that time the strike lost its strength; strikers gradually returned to their work, and on the 24th of June it was officially declared "called off".
> [Italics added]

What Starnes neglected to mention was that the Mounted Police arrived at a gallop swinging baseball bats. Nor is there any convincing evidence from any of the reliable historical sources that shots were fired or missiles thrown before the police galloped through the crowd clubbing people. The statement about the killed and wounded being "foreigners," aside from being incorrect, pinpoints the prejudice of Superintendent Starnes.

The RCMP carried on and improved upon the strike-breaking tradition of their predecessors from the time they were officially founded in 1920. Over the next two decades they played such an important role in labour disputes that some labour experts have claimed they had a profound effect on the attitudes of working people towards the state in Canada. In his 1968 study of labour unrest for the federal Task Force on Labour Relations, Professor Stuart Jamieson asserts that the role of the RCMP helped to generate a distrust for the federal government among trade unionists:

> The RCMP has thus become a highly pervasive force in Canadian society. Its presence has been felt with enough force to tip the scales of battle in hundreds of strikes and labour demonstrations. The particular image of the RCMP, and the federal government itself, which this situation has generated in the eyes of many in the ranks of organized labour, in all probability has had a profound effect on the climate of labour relations in this country.[24]

Alan Phillips, who wrote *The Living Legend* in 1954 and dedicated it to "those officers and men of the Royal Canadian Mounted Police who helped so much with the researching of this book," describes in his book a scene that took place in 1919 as a portent of things to come. It concerns the return to Canada of the Mounted Police squadron from Siberia:

> The RNWMP had done no more than make a few patrols out of Vladivostok. They were gratified, nevertheless, to see a crowd on the Vancouver wharf carrying banners that said: Welcome Home Returning Heroes.
> As they stepped down the gangplank a man tossed a brick, the signal for a barrage of stones. The crowd, the Mounties learned later, were longshoremen. They had read in the newspapers that the RNWMP had been sent home to suppress strikes in Western Canada. The welcome signs, it

turned out, were for the Seaforth Highlanders, who had just come back from France.[25]

Chapter 4
The battle against radicalism

The Security and Intelligence branch (S & I) also known as the "Special Branch" or "Security Services," has been an extremely important part of the RCMP since the modern Force came into being in 1919. Many of the highest ranking officers in the Force, including present Commissioner W. L. Higgitt, have worked in the S & I. Prior to World War I, secret service work in Canada was usually done by the Dominion Police, assisted from time to time by private detective firms contracted by the Department of Justice and other departments of the federal government. While helping the Dominion Police and the civil branch of the Canadian Military Police to enforce the War Measures Act and the Military Service Act during World War I, however, the Mounted Police began to establish an extensive undercover network of their own. This involved mainly investigating, harassing and apprehending socialists, pacifists, labour agitators, draft dodgers and "enemy aliens." Immediately after the war the RNWMP greatly expanded their undercover operations, and when the RCMP was founded they absorbed most of the security and intelligence apparatus formerly under the dominion and military police.

The use of private detective agencies and police spies by both employers and the government during the period of intense unrest after World War I became notorious in labour circles. Quite often in fact, the same detective firm might be working simultaneously for an employer and the government during a strike. Close collaboration between private and public police was common, and sometimes detective agencies worked under direct contract to the RCMP. Their jobs were by no means limited to gathering intelligence on the activities of labour and political activists with the idea that such information might be used by the Crown in prosecutions. They also played an active role in disrupting unions and breaking strikes by both legal and illegal means. They were skillful at sowing dissension within unions and at provoking acts of violence which would provide the police with an excuse to move in and arrest trade union militants. One of the most notorious firms was Pinkerton's Detective Agency, which was used widely in the United States but was also employed in Canada by private employers, the RCMP and other federal agencies. J. S. Woodsworth cited in the House of Commons examples of the kinds of instructions given to spies during strikes:

> We want you to stir up as much bad feeling as you possibly can between the Italians and the Serbians. Spread data among the Serbians that the Italians are going back to work. Call up every question you can in reference to racial hatred between these two nationalities.[1]

Labour leaders had to expend tremendous effort in counteracting the effects of this type of espionage, for instance by warning union members against being tricked into acts of violence by provocateurs. "I should like to assure this House that, in labour circles, when any man stands up at a meeting and begins to talk violence he is immediately suspected by the labour people of being a spy."[2]

The RCMP were using labour spies extensively at the time of the 1919 Winnipeg General Strike, to spy not only on the strike organization in Winnipeg but also on the One Big Union (OBU) and other groups throughout western Canada. In *The Living Legend* Alan Phillips boasts that the RCMP had undercover men in nearly every OBU local in the country, and while this may be an exaggeration, it is probably not far wrong. One RCMP spy who gained his reputation at this time was Corporal F. W. Zaneth. Zaneth, who later became an assistant commissioner of the Force, specialized in infiltrating the OBU, the Socialist Party of Canada and other labour and political groups. He was instrumental in gathering much of the information and providing much of the testimony used to frame (in effect) the leaders of the Winnipeg General Strike on charges of seditious conspiracy. The methods of gathering what passed for evidence against these people were both unethical and illegal. Some of the testimony at the trials was bought and paid for by the RCMP; one witness, a Ukrainian immigrant named Daskaluk who had worked as a temporary special agent for the Force, was promised $500 for his testimony.[3] Corporal Zaneth himself engaged in typical tricks of the agent provocateur. He would sell banned literature for instance and then charge the people who had bought it for having it in their possession.

That spying on labour organizations remained one of the main preoccupations of the RCMP for years after the Winnipeg General Strike is obvious from their annual reports and from evidence cited in Parliament. In addition to maintaining its own regular secret service, the Force spent $87,000 for special agents during 1921 alone. Special agents included people who spied for the police on a part-time or free-lance basis as well as professional private detectives hired for particular assignments. In 1922 J. W. Woodsworth cited some of the anti-labour expenses incurred by the RCMP over the past year. His list comprised a remarkable diversity of items, even including what seems to be some undercover work in the United States:

Employers' Detective Agencies, Services and Expenses of operators	$5608.00
Pinkerton's Detective Agency, Services and Expenses of operators	2412.15
The Thiel Detective Service Company, Services and Expenses of operators	1473.92
O.B.U. Activities	234.62
O.B.U. Labour Unrest at Winnipeg	2173.30
Special Duty at Boston and Springfield	190.70
Investigating Bolshevistic and labour conditions	3380.40
Expenses at Prince Albert, agitators and suspects	49.55
Lumber Workers' Industrial Union of the O.B.U.	356.10
Expenses at Edmonton, attending Labour Church	4.00
Bolshevist and Labour conditions	22.10
At Lethbridge, attending a labour meeting	18.86
Agitators and suspects	31.75
At Vancouver, attending Labour meetings	18.86
Self-Determination League	328.80[4]

The primary target for RCMP infiltration during the 1920s and for decades afterwards was the Communist Party of Canada. The number of agents they employed and the amount of money they spent watching Communists will probably never be known. Sergeant John Leopold, we know, was one of the most successful infiltrators in the RCMP. Leopold joined the RNWMP in 1918 and as soon as he had completed his training began infiltrating radical associations. He eventually ended up in the Communist Party, claiming to be a house painter by the name of Jack Esselwein. "Esselwein" became an ardent trade unionist and a dedicated radical. He was an officer of his local union and a delegate to the Labour Council in Regina. Soon he became the first secretary of the Communist Party in Regina and one of the most prominent activists in Saskatchewan. He was a confidant of the national leaders and later moved on to work out of Winnipeg and Toronto. He successfully spied on his colleagues for eight years before a series of chance occurrences in 1927 and 1928 revealed him to be an RCMP agent. Leopold then dropped out of sight and was transferred to regular police duties in the Yukon. He reappeared in 1931 to supply much of the information and testimony used to convict Tim Buck and seven other prominent Communist leaders under the infamous Section 98 of the Criminal Code.

The prosecution of leaders of the Communist Party in the autumn of 1931 was directed by Attorney-General W. H. Price of Ontario in collaboration with federal authorities and the RCMP. Tim Buck and his colleagues were not charged with any specific conspiracy to overthrow the political and economic system by force.[5] Under Section 98 no such charge was necessary. For merely *belonging* to an association that believed that armed revolution was justifiable a man could be imprisoned for up to 20 years. The prosecution reasoned that, since the Communist Party believed world revolution to be inevitable, it was an unlawful association and its members were guilty of violating Section 98, whether or not they had committed or conspired to commit any specific revolutionary act. The prosecution won the day, Tim Buck and most of his colleagues got sentences of five years in the penitentiary, and the Communist Party became thereby in effect illegal. Frank Scott, the noted constitutional and civil rights lawyer from McGill University, pointed out at the time that the verdict placed Canada on a footing with many of the most repressive governments in the world:

> Only in Italy, Japan, Poland and some of the more reactionary Balkan states is the party completely outlawed. By the Toronto verdict Canada has allied herself with this group of select reactionaries. She is the only country amongst them which claims to be a democracy.[6]

The involvement of the RCMP and Sergeant Leopold in prosecuting Communists led to some interesting questions in police ethics. If Communism was considered illegal by the authorities, then Leopold and others like him must have been guilty of breaking the law. As a prominent Communist activist under the name of Esselwein, Leopold had sold literature, organized meetings and recruited people to the party. Was he not then guilty of counselling people to commit what the authorities defined as a crime? Similarly, weren't all police and private agents who posed as militant advocates of violence and then assisted prosecuting those who followed their advice guilty? Such questions obviously neither interested nor bothered the RCMP. After helping to stomp out "Reds" at the 1931 trials Leopold took up duties at the Ottawa headquarters of the Intelligence Branch. He was later an important figure behind the scenes in the espionage trials and accompanying witch-hunts of 1946, and retired in 1952 with the rank of superintendent.

One of the main reasons for prosecuting the Communist leaders in 1931 and later was to make it hard for them to organize trade unionists and the unemployed under the auspices of the Workers' Unity League.[7]

Many Communists and other radicals were kept so busy defending themselves in the courts that they had little time and few resources for anything else. The RCMP annual report for the year ending September 30, 1932, noted: "The party here is badly in need of funds, and their chief cry at the present time (through the Canadian Labour Defence League) is money and more money for the defence of Communists who are ordered deported."[8]

During the 1930s police agents were constantly on the lookout for critics of the status quo among the unemployed and were placed in nearly every major relief camp as a matter of course. Occasionally an agent surfaced, after a major disturbance, to give testimony at a trial. For instance, Constable H. M. Wilson, who had been placed in a camp on the outskirts of Saskatoon in the spring of 1933, testified at the trial of several people charged after a riot provoked by the police in front of the camp.[9] Reference to police spies among the unemployed occurs frequently in the correspondence of federal Cabinet ministers in the 1930-1935 period. It is clear that many of them were provocateurs.

In a letter to R. B. Bennett in 1934, Saskatchewan Attorney-General M. A. MacPherson related a story told to him by Assistant Commissioner Wood of the RCMP.[10] The story concerned an RCMP agent in Dundurn relief camp who posed as a Communist and denounced the government, only to be told by the other inmates to shut up or they'd throw him out of the camp. MacPherson related the story as an example of the loyalty and contentment of the Dundurn inmates, but it could have been that the inmates suspected the man of being a spy and simply outwitted him.

Many of the people the authorities used as stool pigeons in the relief camps were the same type of lumpen proletarians used to buttress the status quo the world over. Correspondence between the Hon. W. A. Gordon, federal minister of labour, and Brigadier-General Alex Ross, provincial president of the Canadian Legion in Saskatchewan, is revealing in this respect. Ross described an interview he held with the inmates of a temporary relief camp operated by the Canadian Legion.

They have given no trouble at all and responded enthusiastically to my appeal for continued support of constituted law and authority. As a matter of fact when I asked them for suggestions as to what I might do for them the spokesmen suggested that they would be glad to receive uniforms and authority to proceed to clean up the agitators who are at present disturbing the unemployed throughout the country.[11]

Gordon brought the letter to the attention of Major General A. G. L. McNaughton, chief of the General Staff, and asked his opinion on whether such men should be left in one camp or dispersed to various camps "to form a nucleus of safe, dependable men in each camp."[12] The men in question were transferred to the large Dundurn relief camp when it was established by the military authorities in the spring of 1933. There they probably formed a nucleus of "dependables" to stir up the general camp population.

The S & I were (and still are) active in dealing with immigrants. They were responsible for investigating, arresting and incarcerating people scheduled for deportation. It was often the findings of the RCMP investigators that determined whether or not an individual would be deported. The RCMP also investigated immigrants applying for naturalization and had a considerable influence on whether applicants would be granted citizenship. These activities gave the RCMP considerable power over immigrants, and they were by no means averse to using this power to intimidate anyone with radical or even reformist political ideas. In fact they sometimes used their power over immigrants to intimidate them into acting as political stool pigeons in return for a promise of obtaining citizenship or escaping deportation. Sidney Katz reported such a case in an article in *Maclean's*, April 20, 1963. A Finnish woman who had had her citizenship application denied concluded that her membership in a left-wing ethnic association was probably the reason, and since she belonged for cultural rather than political purposes she discontinued her membership. Later S & I agents approached her and suggested she would have a better chance of obtaining her citizenship on the second application if she agreed to rejoin the ethnic association and act as a stool pigeon for the RCMP. She declined.

From the beginning the S & I operators conceived of their job as being nothing less than to maintain the political "purity" of Canada. This meant that any individuals or groups of people who were opposed to the capitalist system or any aspect of it might be subjected to RCMP surveillance, harassment and intimidation. An illustration of how broadly the RCMP interpreted their role is the extent to which they harrassed and attempted to intimidate J. S. Woodsworth and his followers. It was well known in the 1920s that Woodsworth firmly believed, some said to the point of naivety, that basic reforms could be and should be achieved by peaceful and constitutional means. A devout pacifist, Woodsworth even discouraged mass demonstration for fear they would lead to violent confrontations. Nevertheless he and his colleagues did not escape the attentions of the RCMP. Woodsworth cited examples of what he had had to contend with in a speech in the House of Commons in 1922:

... One of the most serious facts in the labour situation is the constant surveillance which labour men, as such, are forced to endure. I should not like to suggest how many thousands of dollars I have cost Canada in having the police trail me around. I want to make that very clear; possibly I was worth watching. But the things I am saying to-day are the very things for which I was trailed, and my fellow-citizens in Winnipeg have very clearly given their verdict as to what they think of this sort of business. I remember a few instances particularly. Before I threw myself into the labour movement I could hardly credit this kind of thing. I remember addressing one night a meeting of labour people, and the next morning an officer of the Mounted Police came to my home and asked me to go to his office. You speak about this as a civil police force. Well, when I entered the office I found everything exactly as though it were a military tribunal. There was an effort made to persuade or intimidate me into either retracting my statements or pledging myself not to make similar statements to the people. I was trying to plead for decency and good order in this country, and to prevent the occasions of strife which are so frequently occurring. I remember speaking at a little town in southern Saskatchewan. The local clergyman was chairman of the meeting, and everything was conducted in perfect good order. But the next day after I left, the local clergyman was subjected to all sorts of indignities at the hands of the local Mounted Police officer. The clergyman happened to have been born in England. He had to tell the Mounted Police officer when he came over to this country, whether he had any connections with the Reds, and Labour, and all the rest of it. A few days later I happened to be addressing a class in political economy in the University of Saskatchewan, and the Mounted Police tried to discover what was going on inside the class room. It was too much for the editor of the local newspaper who reported the address, and he had to reprimand the police and ask what right they had to enter the class rooms of our universities to find out what was being taught. I can remember another occasion at Nanaimo, where a police officer deliberately attempted to draw me into a dispute and to provoke me into saying something that, I presume, he thought would be of service to him.[13]

If pacifists and moderate reformers received this type of treatment, we can imagine what Communists and others who actually believed in revolution had to put up with. As early as the 1920's it was clear that the RCMP, particularly the Intelligence Branch, had become a law unto itself and a menace to political liberty. That menace continues to this day.

Chapter 5
Policing the Depression

Paradoxically, the RCMP force grew rapidly in size and power during the Great Depression of the 1930s, mainly because some of the provinces were in such dire financial trouble that in order to economize they disbanded their police forces and contracted the RCMP to act as provincial police. Many of Canada's smaller municipalities did likewise. This practice continued, until today the RCMP act not only as federal police but also as provincial police and often municipal police as well in all provinces except Ontario and Quebec. Canada has thus developed a much more powerful and centralized federal police force than the United States, which, though it has federal police agencies like the FBI, has none with the scope of the RCMP. Many people have felt this concentration of power to be an intolerable threat to liberty in a democratic society. A. R. M. Lower, for instance, said of the Force in a *Maclean's* article in 1957:

> Its service as a municipal and provincial police force brings a dangerous degree of centralization in our police forces. A government that had a long-range vision of popular liberty would not allow it.[1]

Perhaps the "long-range vision" of Canadian governments can be gauged by the fact that the RCMP have become, if anything, more centralized and more powerful in the years since 1957.

One reason the federal government of R. B. Bennett encouraged the expansion of the RCMP in the early 1930s was that, in a period of economic disaster and mounting unrest, they saw them as the most reliable force in the country for breaking strikes, smashing radical trade unions, controlling the unemployed and hounding political dissenters. In 1932 Prime Minister Bennett cited the alleged "threat to the social order" as a reason for increasing the strength of the RCMP.[2]

To understand the role of the RCMP in the 1930s, one must appreciate the political psychology of the time. Most strikes

58

then were of a desperate character in that they were called to prevent wage cuts and gain some degree of union recognition and job security rather than to achieve significant economic gains. Many employers beset by declining profits took advantage of the high unemployment to reduce wage rates and in many cases to destroy trade unions altogether. This in turn compelled working people to adopt more militant strategies and to seek more radical political solutions to their problems. During this same period thousands of the unemployed were organized into militant unions and associations for the first time, often under the leadership of Communists and other radicals. Despite the fact that the Communist Party had been made in effect illegal by Section 98 of the Criminal Code, the influence of the party grew because of the terrible economic conditions. These conditions also gave rise to the founding of the Co-operative Commonwealth Federation (CCF) in 1932 and to massive extra-parliamentary protest actions in the form of large and frequent demonstrations of the unemployed.

If the federal government was to keep order throughout the country they had to either bring about drastic reforms in the economy and undertake massive government spending to provide employment or resort to political repression on an unprecedented scale. The government did undertake some public works and provide assistance to provincial and municipal relief programs, but it did not mount an attack on the Depression on anywhere near the scale required. The government chose not to undertake large scale expenditures mainly because they still believed in pre-Keynesian economics and did not wish to interfere with private interests. Government leaders feared that massive borrowing would undermine the credit rating of the country and they did not want to compete with private corporate interests in national and international money markets. R. B. Bennett cited credit ratings as the reason for not embarking on additional relief works in 1931: "To maintain our credit, we must practice the most rigid economy and not needlessly spend a single cent."[3] Even as late as the spring of 1935, after Bennett had decided to attempt to regulate the economy, the government was still refusing to undertake massive expenditures on public works as a means of alleviating the unemployment problem. Defence Minister George Perley admitted that the government was being besieged by "responsible citizens" to undertake a major public works program but refused to do so on the grounds that it might harm the private sector of the economy:

It might result in compromising the orderly revival of industry, which at present is progressing hopefully. Every undue burden of this character which is assumed lessens the rate at which recovery will take place.[4]

From the beginning of the Depression it was clear that the poorest and least powerful sectors of the population would be expected to make the greatest sacrifices. Employed workers would be expected to accept wage reductions and deteriorating working conditions, and the unemployed would be expected to eke out an existence on next to nothing in the interests of the "credit rating" of the country. They did not accept this situation sitting down. Strikes became frequent and bitter, and demonstrations of the unemployed ever more militant. The response of the federal government and their supporters was to blame all unrest and disorder on "Reds," "foreigners" and all the other elements allegedly involved in some fanatical conspiracy against Christian civilization. Such scapegoats both deflected people's attention from the injustices of the system and justified increased authoritarianism. The situation soon polarized into those people who defended the status quo and those who demanded basic changes in the economic system or at the very least a major government-sponsored work and wages program to alleviate the suffering of the unemployed. Stuart Jamieson has described the results of this polarization: "The participation of unemployed groups in demonstrations and riots brought civil disturbance generally to a new high and provoked the most widespread, severe and in many cases brutal measures of repression by police forces since the Winnipeg General Strike."[5]

In an attempt to discredit their critics, the Establishment launched a saturation propaganda campaign depicting the country as being in basically sound shape except for the threat allegedly posed by communistic foreigners. They singled out European immigrants for vilification, the very people an earlier propaganda campaign by the government and the CPR had encouraged to come to Canada when farmers and workers were badly needed to open up the country and provide cheap labour for the railway's and the mining and forestry industries. They had worked for years in the least desirable jobs at less than average wages, and now that they were unemployed in the thousands, they were victimized and used as scapegoats to explain the lack of jobs for the population as a whole. In their campaign against radicals, the authorities could also exploit popular prejudices against non-Anglo-Saxons by portraying socialism as an un-Canadian or un-British philosophy perpetrated by supposedly unpatriotic foreigners.

Some of the most tireless and most rabid of the right-wing, racist demagogues of the 1930s happened to be prominent judges and high-ranking police officers. One was Chief Justice William Mulock of Ontario, considered at the time to be one of Canada's elder statesmen. In Toronto's Royal York Hotel on February 4, 1931, Sir William made an after-dinner speech to an audience of 1,000 stock-breeders and exhibitors who were guests of the Canadian National Exhibition in which he portrayed Communists as conspirators, implied that many immigrants were Communists, and prescribed appropriate action for Canada to take:

> If Canada is content to have her laws made by those who deny the existence of God, who would suppress religion, who would destroy the sacredness of marriage and who would nationalize women, who would extinguish the love of parents, who would deprive children in their tender years of a mother's care and expose them to the imminent danger of growing up as criminals; who would rob all citizens by any degree of force up to that of murder, of all their worldly goods and leave them penniless; who would make it a crime for one to save; would deprive people of liberty and would make slaves of them to the State.
>
> If, I say, those are the conditions which Canada is content to have established in Canada then let her open her doors wide and admit into full citizenship the millions of the people of that class.
>
> But if Canada does not wish to become a hell on earth she should rid herself at once of those who would, if they could, make her such, and let her prevent any of that kind of people ever setting foot on Canadian soil.[6]

Mulock's speech was widely reported in the daily press and editorialists lauded him as "an elder statesman who has given a lifetime of service to the state; he has nothing but the welfare of the state in mind."[7] They said the audience had applauded the speech wildly and listed among the enthusiastic head table guests the Hon. Leopold Macaulay, Ontario provincial secretary; the Hon. Gideon Robertson, federal minister of labour; Judge Emerson Coatsworth, chairman of the Toronto board of police commissioners; Toronto Police Chief D. C. Draper; and Canon H. J. Cody, chairman of the board of governors of the University of Toronto.

Unfortunately Sir William Mulock was not an anomaly among the judiciary, though few of his colleagues could match him in oratorical invective. Even further right than Mulock was Magistrate S. Alfred Jones, K.C., who delivered an address entitled "Fascism" before the Empire Club of Canada in Toronto on January 25, 1934. After describing in glowing terms the great things Fascism had done for Italy, Jones ended his speech on this staggering note:

> If there were a line in the fundamental principles of Fascism, opposed in the slightest degree to the best ideals of the British Empire, I would not even be discussing the matter. Should Canada at any time in the future, in its wisdom, adopt Fascism, in whole or in part, it is indeed gratifying to know, gentlemen, that the system fits so admirably into our Imperial setting, and that the old flag would still be ours and that the song of Empire, "God Save the King", would still be that of Canada. (Hearty applause.)[8]

The Empire Club comprised Canada's political, business and professional elite. The governor-general was honorary president, and life members included people like Sir Robert Borden. Considering the political climate of the time, the situation suggested in Jones's concluding statement was perhaps all too possible.

If certain members of the judiciary appeared extreme in their pronouncements, Major-General James H. MacBrien, commissioner of the RCMP, proved time and again that he was second to nobody when it came to identifying the problems of the Depression and prescribing solutions for them. A former chief of staff, MacBrien was appointed commissioner in 1931 and served until his death in 1938. Given the duties of the Force during the 1930s, it was perhaps appropriate that a man who had spent most of his life in the military should be appointed commissioner, and MacBrien brought with him from the army a reputation of being "trigger happy" in his reactions to strikes and industrial unrest. He expanded the RCMP by nearly 1,000 men during his first year of office and made it even more military in character than it had been previously.

The new commissioner was soon pronouncing on how to solve the unemployment problem. In a speech to a Vimy night gathering in Toronto in 1932, he blamed unemployment on the communists:

It is notable that 99% of these fellows are foreigners and many of them have not been here long. The best thing to do would be to send them back where they came from in every way possible. *If we were rid of them there would be no unemployment or unrest in Canada.*[9] [Italics added]

The *Mail and Empire* quoted MacBrien in the same speech as expressing approval of an offer by certain returned men "to turn out *en masse* to suppress the Reds."[10] This speech was too much for many people and drew criticism from parts of the press and in Parliament. The *Canadian Forum* was aghast at the irresponsibility of it and wondered what the RCMP was coming to:

No one wants to see the force turned into a sort of Fascist Militia. Fortunately all further comment on the alleged remarks of General MacBrien is rendered superfluous by the few words of wisdom that came from the lips of the chairman at the same banquet. He was speaking on the general subject of casualties and, according to the *Mail and Empire*, concluded his remarks as follows: "The rest of you who look all right are also affected. If you were not damaged physically you were mentally . . . I know I'm crazy more or less and I know I'm speaking facts and not insults when I say that the rest of you are pretty much the same way."[11]

MacBrien remained undaunted in the face of such comments. By 1935 he was publicly advocating that people set up vigilante groups to assist the RCMP in fighting the "Reds."

The speeches of Commissioner MacBrien may seem ridiculous today, but the actions of the RCMP during the 1930s were no laughing matter. The Force did much of the dirty work for the immigration authorities in deporting thousands of immigrants. Under the Immigration Act, an immigrant who had been in Canada less than five years could be deported should he or she become a "public charge." The significant provision of the Act was that they *could* be deported if the authorities chose to act. This meant that anyone in this category who was on relief, for instance, would be afraid to criticize relief policies for fear of deportation. The Immigration Act also provided that anyone not born in the country, regardless of how long he had lived in Canada, could be deported for advocating overthrow by force of constituted authority "or by word or act creating or attempting to create riot or public disorder in Canada."

The authorities often preferred to deport people rather than try them under Section 98 or some other statute, because it avoided the necessity of a public trial. A person scheduled for deportation was entitled to be represented by a lawyer but was given no hearing in open court. His case could be appealed to an internal committee of the Department of Immigration, but the hearing was held in camera. Men could be, and sometimes were, arrested by the RCMP in the middle of the night and sent by train to Halifax, where they were imprisoned in the immigration sheds pending disposal of their case by the Department of Immigration.[12] Thousands of miles from relatives and friends, they would find it very difficult to obtain the services of lawyers and other assistance. One example cited by J. S. Woodsworth in the House of Commons involved three men, Daniel Holmes (Chomirki), Orton Wade and Konrad Cessinger, who were seized by RCMP in Winnipeg without warrant and transported to Halifax to await deportation.[13] Although the three were known radicals, they had no police records, and one had been in Canada for 20 years and had a Canadian wife and child.

The case of the three Winnipeg men was by no means atypical. The extent to which deportations increased during the 1930s was astonishing. Between 1903 and 1928 a total of 27,660 immigrants were deported, an average of slightly more than 1,000 annually; then the rate began to rise rapidly with the onset of the Depression in 1929, and in 1931 alone 7,000 were deported.

On October 13, 1931, the minister of justice called a special meeting in his office to discuss the need to increase the number of deportations.[14] In attendance were the acting minister of justice, the minister of national defence and the commissioner of immigration, the chief of the general staff and Commissioner MacBrien of the RCMP. They decided that deportation facilities were insufficient and agreed that the army would turn Melville Island Barracks at Halifax over to the

RCMP to be used as a detention centre for persons awaiting deportation.

The most common cause cited for deportations was that the people in question were "public charges." No separate figures were published for the number of people deported for political reasons, but even a conservative estimate would put them in the hundreds during the 1930-1935 period. The government deported many socialists and communists to countries with fascist or military dictatorships, where they would be imprisoned or executed upon arrival. The *Canadian Forum* documented at least one case of a man deported from Canada to Germany who died in a Nazi concentration camp.[15]

Rounding up people for deportation was only one of the tasks of the RCMP in the early 1930s. They arrested Communists under Section 98 of the Criminal Code, as described in the previous chapter. They were also active in breaking up demonstrations of the unemployed and outdoor political rallies, often in conjunction with provincial and municipal police. A perusal of the newspapers and personal accounts of the period indicates that many, perhaps most, riots were provoked by the police, who would attempt to disperse peaceful parades or mass meetings with nightsticks or who would ride through crowds on horseback attacking people with clubs. The RCMP usually followed up these events with arrests, fines, jail sentences and sometimes deportation. Stuart Jamieson has described the situation that prevailed in Vancouver:

> The married unemployed were given relief by means of a "gunny sack parade" at which married men lined up in front of an old church building on the Cambie Street grounds to receive their quota of food and tokens exchangeable for shelter and fuel. Mass meetings on the grounds, parades, and protest marches to City Hall by the unemployed, were attacked repeatedly by forces from the RCMP, the provincial police, and a specially trained "riot squad" of mounted city police armed with long, lead-weighted clubs. There were numerous serious riots in which hundreds were injured in Vancouver during the first few years of the Great Depression.[16]

Every May Day police would break up dozens of parades and rallies in cities and towns across the country. It would be almost impossible to ascertain the total number of arrests for what could be called political offences during the 1930s, but surely the number would be in the thousands. An article by Beckie Buhay in the *Canadian Labour Defender* of August 1932 listed all of the arrests and convictions for the past year. Buhay claimed that there had been 720 arrests and 155 convictions for political offences during 1931. She also asserted that there had been 556 more arrests and 33 political deportations since the beginning of 1932, and that 49 more political activists were being held for deportation. We cannot know for certain if Buhay's statistics were exact, but judging from scattered local reports in other newspapers and journals and questions in Parliament, they were probably reasonably accurate.

The general use of police spies within political, labour and unemployed associations has been discussed in the previous chapter. In many cases the authorities used information obtained by these agents to assist employers in breaking strikes and destroying unions. During the 1930s there was also collaboration between government officials and "citizens' committees" of the type used at the time of the Winnipeg General Strike and some encouragement of the kind of vigilante groups publicly advocated by Commissioner MacBrien. An amendment to the RCMP Act in 1932 gave the commissioner the power to "appoint without pay special groups publicly advocated by Commissioner MacBrien. An amendment to the RCMP constables ... for a period not exceeding twelve months at any one time for the purpose of maintaining law and order at the request of any department of the government." The amendment was criticized in the House of Commons by Ernest Lapointe and J. S. Woodsworth on the grounds that it could be used to give company officials police powers against their own employees. The amendment fitted nicely into MacBrien's philosophy on the role of the RCMP.

One example of official collaboration with private employers against radical trade unionists was a meeting in May 1935, attended by the following: J. O. Apps, general executive assistant of the CPR; C. A. Cottrill, assistant general manager, B. C. District of the CPR; Major-General A. G. L. McNaughton, chief of the general staff; and Major G. R. Turner.[17] The subjects under discussion at the meeting were the need to co-ordinate employer-government actions designed to frustrate an expected strike of longshoremen and steps needed to combat radical trade unionists in general on the West Coast. Among the topics discussed were the availability of Canadian Pacific boats to transport troops from Victoria to

Vancouver in the event of major trouble and the setting up of a "Five Hundred Club" of Vancouver businessmen "along the lines of similar citizens' vigilance committees in cities along the Pacific Coast of the U.S.A."[18] A confidential memorandum describing the meeting was forwarded to a number of government officials including Commissioner MacBrien.

Prime Minister Bennett agreed that the RCMP and other law enforcement agencies should be put at the service of right-wing extremists, and said so in a correspondence with Alex Lockwood, president of the Anti-Communist League of Flin Flon, Manitoba, dated June and July, 1935.[19] Lockwood had written to Bennett to describe the activities of the league and to appeal for stronger government measures against the "undesirable elements" in the country. He described the Anti-Communist League as "a non-political non-sectarian organization. It stands for the ruthless suppression of Communism in all its forms." Lockwood then described the league's activities as being devoted mainly to ridding Flin Flon of "foreigners" and Communists. League members were planning to organize throughout the country and were willing to break the law if necessary in the struggle against the "Reds." "Should our activities bring us into contact with the law," wrote Lockwood, "we still shall not hesitate as we deem Canada to be in dire peril at the present moment and no sacrifice any of us may make will be considered too great a price, if it in turn preserves our Country from the Red Menace." Lockwood then went on to demand more vigorous action by the authorities against unnamed individuals whom he describes as being "foreigners" responsible for Communistic agitation in the Flin Flon area. We might expect that Bennett, who was constantly making speeches about law and order, would have considered Lockwood a threat to the public peace and cautioned him to stay within the law or perhaps even requested the RCMP to investigate the activities of the league. Instead Bennett offered the co-operation of the government and encouraged Lockwood to continue his efforts:

> You should communicate with the Attorney-General of Manitoba, as under our Constitution, matters of this kind come under his jurisdiction. However, if you will send me in confidence the names of those to whom you refer I will

ascertain whether or not it is possible to deport them as undesirables.

The prime minister ended his letter, "congratulating you upon your fine sense of public duty as a citizen of Canada." Clearly Bennett applied the term "law and order" differently to different people.

A full description of RCMP involvement in strikes during the 1930s would require at least an entire volume in itself.[20] We will deal here very briefly with some of their activities in the mining regions where some of the bitterest labour battles of the Depression were fought. Coal miners suffered repeated wage cuts and frequent layoffs, and the fact that many lived in company towns made their exploitation doubly vicious. Labour historians have described how rebellions against working and living conditions and attempts by miners to gain union recognition invariably led to reprisals by the companies and the forces of the state:

> In general, the record of the years 1930 to 1935 in coal mining is a monotonous recital of dozens of strikes and arrests in the hundreds. Strikers were arrested, not just for violence, but for such minor reasons as violation of the I.D.I. Act (i.e., going on strike without first applying for conciliation). In many cases, the purposes of the arrests were revealed by the withdrawal of charges as soon as the strikes were ended.[21]

One union which had great difficulty in gaining recognition from employers and governments was the Mine Workers' Union of Canada (MWUC). The MWUC was affiliated to the Workers' Unity League (WUL), a Communist-led union federation organized in 1930. Governments and employers hated the MWUC with an unbelievable vehemence and would go to almost any lengths to deny it recognition as the bargaining agent for miners. While this opposition was ostensibly on the grounds that the MWUC was part of the "international Communist conspiracy," the more important reason as far as employers were concerned was that the MWUC was one of the few unions during this period to put up a sustained fight against falling wages and deteriorating conditions in the mine fields. As a result there was a concerted effort by employers, backed up by the federal government, to destroy the union despite the fact that it was supported by the great majority of miners in several mining regions of Alberta and British Columbia and some in other provinces. The smashing of this union was accompanied by some of the most brutal atrocities in Canadian labour history. Stuart Jamieson has described one violent incident which took place during a coal miners' strike in Corbin, British Columbia, in 1935:

> The miners and their wives, 250 in all, paraded to the mine, where they were met by a large detachment of police and strike-breakers on a narrow ledge from which there was no escape. When the women formed themselves into a picket line, the police drove a bulldozer into the gathering, breaking the limbs of several women. Further violence ensued, in which it was reported that 16 policemen and 25 strikers were injured. Seventeen strikers, including the president and secretary of the union, were arrested.[22]

Additional RCMP reinforcements then moved into the area and blocked off roads so miners in outlying regions could not come to the assistance of their brothers in Corbin.

One of the famous strikes of this period which has been studied in some detail was a coal miners' strike in the Bienfait-Estevan area of Saskatchewan in 1931. The mine owners flatly refused to recognize or meet with the union; some of them attempted to break the strike by bringing in scabs under police protection. On September 29, the tragic Estevan riot occurred. Three miners were killed by police bullets and eight were wounded. Four bystanders and one policeman were also wounded by bullets and nine police personnel were injured. There were probably many more injuries to civilians which were never reported. The causes and events of this riot have since been a subject of great controversy between those who lay the blame entirely on the Estevan authorities and the police and those who blame the miners and their leaders. The most detailed and authoritative account of the events of September 29, 1931, is contained in S. D. Hanson's *The Estevan Strike and Riot, 1931* (an unpublished M.A. thesis, University of Saskatchewan, Regina Campus, 1971). Hanson had no axe to grind for either side and took pains to be scrupulously objective. He found that, although no one was blameless, the major blame lay with the Estevan town authorities and that the RCMP members on the scene probably overreacted. Hanson also found that subsequent to the riot the local and provincial authorities as well as the police and judiciary acted in a biased, dishonest and, in some cases, unlawful manner.

The events leading to the bloody confrontation in Estevan began with the miners deciding to parade through the town on September 29 as an advertisement for a rally that evening in the town hall. The town council prohibited the parade and the use of the hall for an evening rally. Hanson asserts that this was a foolish decision which greatly increased the possibility of violence:

> Parades and demonstrations designed to dramatize the plight of miners and acquire support in their fights for improved wages and working conditions are common throughout the coal mining regions of North America. Had Council issued a permit to the striking miners to demonstrate, it is unlikely that any violence or loss of life would have resulted. Although the situation in the Souris coalfield was tense, it would appear that the town authorities overreacted in banning the parade.

Informed of the ban on the parade, the miners' committee decided to proceed with a car cavalcade on the grounds that the technicality of whether a car cavalcade was in fact a parade might get around the ban. In any event the miners were in the mood to defy the ban if necessary.

About 200 miners with their wives and children assembled in Bienfait in the early afternoon and proceeded in a cavalcade towards Estevan. They planned to confront Mayor Bannatyne and demand that he rescind the prohibition on the evening meeting. More people joined them along the way, so that by the time they reached Estevan at 3 P.M. they numbered about 400. In the vicinity that day were the Estevan city police and 13 special company police in addition to 47 RCMP under the command of Inspector Moorhead. The RCMP were well equipped with 30 rifles, 48 revolvers, 48 riding crops and 4 machine guns.[23] When the cavalcade reached Estevan, only about 20 of the police were in the town. The others, under Inspector Moorhead, were a few miles away at the Truax-Traer mines, where they expected the miners might take action against the scabs. A cordon of police stopped the cavalcade at Fourth Street and Eleventh Avenue, near the town hall and the court house. A fight broke out between Estevan Police Chief McCutcheon and a miner named Martin Day. People from both sides joined in the ensuing struggle, and what amounted to a riot was soon in progress. The police commandeered a fire engine to hose the men down, but the miners captured it. When a miner named Nick Norgan grabbed a fire-fighting axe and attempted to smash the machine, he was shot through the heart by a policeman and died instantly. This enraged the crowd, and they fought the police with increased fury until Inspector Moorhead arrived from Truax-Traer with about 30 more RCMP and dispersed them.

That night Estevan resembled an armed fortress. An additional 45 RCMP arrived from Regina, and sentries with machine guns were set up at strategic locations throughout the town. The Estevan militia was called out, and arrangements were made to call out the Winnipeg Strathconas if necessary. The next day 60 RCMP, armed to the teeth, with a machine gun mounted on a patrol wagon, searched homes in Bienfait. They arrested 13 people that day, and 13 more in the next few weeks, including Annie Buller, a well-known strike leader. Most of these people were tried on charges of rioting, assaulting and wounding police officers and unlawful assembly, and most were found guilty. Some had to pay substantial fines, and others were jailed. Sam Scarlett and Annie Buller were given the longest jail terms — one year each. Annie Buller had been charged with rioting but, according to Hanson, more attention was paid at her trial to a speech she had made at a public rally on September 27 than to her activities on the day of the riot.[24] There was, in fact, no concrete proof that she participated in the riot, though she was with the cavalcade at the time.[25] Not a single policeman was charged or even reprimanded for killing and wounding miners and bystanders.

In the weeks following September 29, the authorities and the police carried on a deceitful campaign to exonerate themselves and discredit the strikers. They spread the story that the strike leaders had been informed that the police intended to break up the parade, but that they purposely kept the miners in the dark about it. They also claimed that when the miners arrived in Estevan they were armed with clubs and even some guns. But if the miners did not know that the police intended to break up the cavalcade, why would they come armed? And if they did know and intended to make a fight of it, why would they bring their wives and children with them? The police also claimed that the miners initiated the riot without provocation, and that the police did not draw their guns until they had been backed up to the town hall by the crowd and had no other choice.

In preparing his thesis, Hanson sifted through the evidence and attempted to reconstruct what happened in Estevan based on facts and logic rather than on prejudicial testimony.[26] He found that the strike leaders *had not* been informed that the town council had ordered the police to break up the parade but only that the parade had been banned. Hanson concludes that the police were probably not in fact ordered to take action against the cavalcade until the last minute, when it had already reached the outskirts of Estevan. Evidence for this is overwhelming. If the police had intended in advance to break up the parade of miners, why were nearly two-thirds of the RCMP contingent several miles away at Truax-Traer rather than in Estevan? And why would the police wait until the cavalcade had entered Estevan? Why not stop it on the outskirts in order to avoid property damage and injury to bystanders? The most convincing evidence is the two communications sent to the strike leaders. The first, handed to two of the leaders late in the morning on September 29, informed them that the proposed parade and rally had both been banned, but did not mention that the police had been ordered to enforce the ban. The second communication, a letter from the town council to the strike leaders, informed them of the ban on the parade and also stated that the police would stop the parade if the strikers ignored the ban. It was postmarked 10 P.M., September 29, several hours after the riot.

Hanson presents the factual evidence and then offers the only explanation that makes sense. The town council must have passed the motion banning the parade on the morning of September 29 and considered the matter closed. Inspector Moorhead of the RCMP, having heard rumours that there might be trouble at the Truax-Traer mines, took the bulk of his contingent there and left the remainder on call in Estevan. In the afternoon the town authorities heard that the cavalcade was headed towards Estevan and, after hurried consultation, ordered the police to stop it, rather than allowing it to go ahead, meet with the mayor, and perhaps try to work out some sort of compromise on the use of the hall for that evening. By this time the cavalcade was on the outskirts of Estevan, so the police hurriedly threw up their cordon on Fourth Street rather than outside the city. Minutes later all hell broke loose, and when it was over three men were dead and two dozen more were wounded or injured.

Then and there, the police and the local officials got busy constructing the "big lie."

Viewing the carnage, the authorities like normal individuals were doubtless horrified and frightened lest they be regarded as heavily responsible through failure to take necessary steps to head off violence, especially violence in which non-participants had been struck by flying bullets. Under the circumstances they might well panic and begin asking what they could do to make themselves appear as innocent as possible and thereby place as much blame as possible on the miners.[27]

It appears almost certain that what they did (though in retrospect they were none too bright about it) was alter the minutes of the morning council meeting and then send a second communication to the leaders of the miners. The RCMP and city police officials probably co-operated in the falsification of public documents; they certainly spread false information. Hanson points out that there is no account of the meeting of September 29, 1931, in the minute book of the Estevan town council. "All that remains as a record of this meeting is what is purported to be a copy of the minutes filed as an exhibit at the trial of Anne Buller, a document bearing no notation stating that it is either the original or a certified copy of the minutes."[28]

The falsification of documents was only the beginning of the irregularities. RCMP constables and city policemen evidently perjured themselves during the trials of the miners. Several of them swore, for instance, that they did not draw their guns until they were backed up to city hall, whereas photographs of the scene prove otherwise. They also spread the story that Martin Day made a vicious and unprovoked attack on Police Chief McCutcheon, and that the riot started when other miners attacked policemen who were trying to arrest Day. The evidence is not at all clear. One of the defence lawyers accused the police of having "started the riot with their riding crops,"[29] and Hanson agrees that this was a distinct possibility.

It is conceivable that the officers had already provoked the miners or used more force than was necessary to prevent

Day's being freed. If this were in fact the case, only a thin line separates attacker from defender.[30]

Day denied having struck the first blow, and it is noteworthy that when he was tried he was charged only with rioting, *not* with assaulting an officer. The police gave conflicting testimony as to who struck whom first, and a man named Joseph Bernatos, who was with Day at the time, *was* convicted of assaulting a police officer.

Hanson says, it is entirely possible that the police provoked the whole episode. Certainly after the disorder became general the police lost control of themselves and used their guns unnecessarily. Many of the RCMP at Estevan were inexperienced; 34 of the 43 constables had been with the Force less than one year, and many came directly from the training depot in Regina. Was it necessary to kill a man to save a fire engine? And why was at least one man, Pete Markunas, shot "in several places"?[31] The police were never able to prove that any of the miners used guns, though they tried very hard to do so.

The evidence at the trials added up to a complete mockery of justice. One exhibit purporting to be weapons carried by the miners consisted of pieces of lead and iron pipe, axles, shafts and other automobile parts, and an old, broken army rifle. The Regina *Leader-Post* questioned the authenticity of this exhibit: "Judging by the size of some of the weapons, some husky men must have been in the crowd to wield them, or to throw them any distance."[32] Evidence suggests that the police or their collaborators gathered up the "weapons" from an old scrap heap. Defence counsel W. H. Hefferman specifically charged Police Chief McCutcheon with having paid some boys to go out and collect the material; the chief, of course, denied the charge and claimed he had had two constables gather it up from the riot scene.

Hanson points especially to the absurdity of including the old army rifle in the exhibit:

Is it likely that any miner would have transported an old, broken army rifle to Estevan much less have dared to throw such an object at the police? Surely any individual with even a minimal degree of common sense would realize that his chances of being shot by the nearest police officers were exceeding great should he be seen even picking up such a weapon.[33]

Hanson concludes that the miners threw stones, washers, pieces of metal and chunks of wood at the police during the riot, but considers these a far cry from the "armaments" exhibited in court.

Other aspects of the trials were in no way flattering to the authorities. In the case of one man, Roy Buttazoni, the local Estevan police admitted that they had been "out to get" him for some time. There were also attempts to influence the jury by lawyers for the mine owners. One lawyer treated three of the jurors to drinks in a hotel room and declared, in reference to Sam Scarlett and Annie Buller, "We will have to get the whole bunch of red sons of bitches."[34] Before the trials ever commenced, the Saskatchewan attorney-general openly and repeatedly denounced many of the defendants for Communism, radical agitation and similar "crimes." In two of the trials, the presiding judges showed obvious bias in their charges to the jurors.[35]

If the actions of the police, courts and politicians were reprehensible, the actions of some of the leading citizens of Estevan were even worse. Dr. Creighton, who was in charge of the local hospital, testified before the Wylie Commission that he had given orders not to admit wounded miners unless they could pay a week in advance.

> Dr. Creighton stated that he realized there would be some men wounded during the melee so he telephoned his secretary and instructed her not to allow anyone into the hospital unless payment was made to the hospital for a week in advance. The only exceptions were to be men in uniform "because the government pays the medical expenses of their own people". An astonishing order from a man who had been collecting $1.25 a month for a number of years from numerous miners in the area![36]

Creighton's order probably cost the life of Pete Markunas, who died shortly after arriving in Weyburn Hospital, 60 miles from Estevan.

From beginning to end the whole affair was an example of class justice at its worst, and the miners were understandably embittered. The three deceased victims, Nick Norgan, Pete Markunas and Julian Gryshko, were buried by the miners in a common grave in the Bienfait cemetery. A year later the Ukrainian Labor Temple erected a monument on the grave bearing the names of the dead miners along with the inscription *Murdered In Estevan September 29, 1931 By RCMP*. The Bienfait authorities later had the letters "*RCMP*" removed.

The events surrounding the Bienfait-Estevan strike were not at all atypical. Throughout the 1920s and 1930s, similar events occurred in Cape Breton, Sudbury, Flin Flon, Blairmore, Corbin, Vancouver Island and dozens of other districts where men mined for coal and metal. In many instances the activities of the police and other officials were even more reprehensible than in Estevan, but in no other instance were as many men killed.[37] Governments and police and especially the RCMP automatically sided with the employers. The RCMP were used mainly to protect company property and scabs, but they were also often used to intimidate strikers by means of legal or violent action.

The RCMP became such a regular strikebreaking force that, whenever a major strike occurred in the Western provinces, the members expected to see duty in the vicinity. Constable N. J. McKenzie wrote an article entitled "A Strike in the Estevan Coal Fields" for the *RCMP Quarterly* of January 1941, in which he describes another strike in the vicinity in 1939 in which the RCMP were involved:

> On October 25, 1939, telephone lines from headquarters to the detachment men throughout Saskatchewan buzzed with the ominous words, "Stand To, Stand To". We all knew what that meant. We had read in the local papers that the Estevan coal-field miners were again on strike.

McKenzie then describes how he was part of a contingent stationed in the Estevan area for over a month until the strike was settled. Their main job was to protect scabs, a job for which McKenzie saw no need to apologize. There were no incidents of violence in this strike, and McKenzie looked upon it as a social occasion:

> It was a strike enjoyed by everyone; in fact it seemed like a "get together" to make new friendships and renew the old. It will be remembered by all.

If the Bennett government and the RCMP were no friends to those working people fortunate enough to keep their jobs in the early 1930s, they were even less kindly disposed towards the unemployed. We have mentioned how the RCMP were kept busy dispersing demonstrations and harassing unemployed groups. The battleground shifted somewhat in 1932, when the federal government established the infamous relief camps for the single unemployed and began to force young men out of the cities and into the camps, where they were expected to work 44 hours a week for their board plus the princely sum of 20 cents a day.[38] The Department of National Defence operated the camps in an extremely authoritarian manner; it denied the men the most elementary civil rights. The inmates did not take this treatment lying down, but rather organized secret camp committees under the auspices of the Relief Camp Workers' Union (RCWU). Strikes and acts of protest and civil disobedience became common. The RCMP were enlisted to establish an elaborate network of spies in almost every major camp and to arrest agitators. Between 1932 and 1935 they imprisoned scores of RCWU activists and other protesters in the camps.

The single unemployed, however, refused to accept camp conditions and continued to demand work and wages under dignified circumstances. The federal government, refusing to take effective economic measures but fearing that existing conditions would drive the unemployed to agitate further, prepared legislation and made plans for establishing "Camps of Discipline," which were designed to be prison camps for incarcerating any activists deemed a threat to public order.[39] Fortunately the federal government never actually incarcerated people in Camps of Discipline, despite extensive efforts on the part of Commissioner MacBrien of the RCMP. In May 1935, MacBrien was exerting pressure on the government to establish these camps and also to impose complete military discipline on the regular relief camps.[40]

General McNaughton, chief of the general staff, was instrumental in talking the government out of such drastic action.

The RCMP were extremely active during the On-to-Ottawa Trek of the single unemployed which culminated in the Regina riot of July 1, 1935. The RCMP tried to discredit the trekkers and their leaders, they harassed citizens who attempted to assist the trekkers, and they frustrated the government of Saskatchewan, which was vehemently opposed to federal plans to stop the trekkers in Regina at all costs. That the RCMP provoked the riot of July 1 has been proven beyond a doubt.[41] They also helped to follow it up with numerous arrests and a long series of trials. The RCMP and the federal government then embarked upon another campaign of organized deception, but with a little less success than usual. By 1935 the Bennett government and the Force were both losing credibility in the eyes of a very significant segment of the population, but the Force made no effort to reform itself or change its outlook. The man in charge of the dirty work in Regina in 1935 was Assistant Commissioner S. T. Wood. He gained stature in the eyes of Commissioner MacBrien by the way he handled the Trek, was duly promoted and soon became acting deputy commissioner. On the death of MacBrien in 1938, Wood succeeded him as commissioner, a job for which he was eminently suited. He had been trained at Royal Military College, had a reputation for strikebreaking and waging war on "subversives," and was a personal friend and great admirer of J. Edgar Hoover.

The role of the RCMP in suppressing the protests of the underprivileged during the 1930s strongly affected the attitude of many trade union activists towards state authority.

The frequency with which governments invoked force and violence to suppress such action, particularly in breaking up unemployed demonstrations, and in helping employers break strikes, tended to generate an image of government as an oppressor. It perhaps encouraged a widespread contempt for the law as an entity designed to protect property rather than human rights.[42]

The image of the RCMP was permanently tarnished in labour circles and became somewhat less attractive to the population as a whole. The Force responded to this by improved public relations techniques during and after World War II.

The substance of their role would not change, but it would be made more palatable by clever disguises.

Chapter 6
Fascism, Communism and the
RCMP Quarterly

It is in the interests of the rich and powerful in any society in which they exist to perpetuate the prevailing system. The last resort and the crudest instruments of these groups in a democracy are their military and police forces. Because it is the job of the policemen in such societies to defend the status quo against its detractors, the leaders of police forces usually develop a political psychology considerably to the right of society as a whole. In fact the police forces of a liberal democracy often betray an admiration, whether overt or implied, of Fascist and military governments. They also tend to exhibit an almost paranoid fear of Communism, socialism and other "subversive" doctrines which challenge the existing order. This then drives them to demand more power to deal with these "enemies of society," and in that drive for more power they can actually become a threat to the civil liberties of the populace.

That the top policy makers of the RCMP have for several decades displayed the above tendencies is evident not only from the work of the Force during that time but also from the leaders' efforts to inculcate in their men and in the general public a right-wing ideology based on an almost hysterical fear of Communism. This can best be illustrated by an examination of the *RCMP Quarterly* and other official publications of the Force over the past 40 years. Articles dealing with political subjects in the *RCMP Quarterly* have without exception been right-wing in orientation, and often even in the category of the extreme Right.

In common with the extreme Right, the political thinkers of the RCMP believe or purport to believe in the conspiracy theory of history. According to this theory, political unrest and disorder stem from small groups of evil conspirators, usually subservient to a demonic, monolithic leadership. In past centuries Masons, Jews, Jesuits and numerous other religious, ethnic and political groups have often been portrayed as the perpetrators of worldwide disorders and intrigue.

Since the Bolshevik Revolution of 1917, the extreme political Right in most Western countries have generally been obsessed with the "international Communist conspiracy" directed from Moscow and dedicated to the complete destruction of freedom, religion, the family and nearly everything else most people hold sacred. Because this type of political reasoning tends to attract anti-Semites and other unhealthy elements of a population, Jews and other minority groups are usually assigned key roles in the infamous "international conspiracy." When these distortions become a part of the official outlook of the main police force in a country, the unhealthiest sections of the body politic are as good as officially endorsed.

In their campaign against Communists and other radicals during the 1930s, the RCMP maintained a constant propaganda barrage to inform their own members and the public of the dangers of the "Red Menace." In an article in the *RCMP Quarterly* of July 1935, Superintendent E. J. Mead warned that the tentacles of the Communist Party were reaching throughout the land and posing a grave threat to Canadian society. He asserted that nearly all instances of disorder and 90 percent of the strikes in the country were caused by Communists. "This explains why such a militant attitude is so often adopted by those on strike during an industrial dispute." He warned readers that the Communist Party used numerous "front" groups "to bring within its scope those elements who can so often find good in every form of Government, except their own, but who have not the courage to submit to Communist Party discipline." He pointed out that no section of the populace "escapes the Party policy of subversion — even women and children are brought within its influence." He said of the doctrines perpetrated by Communists: "It is in keeping with the teachings of Communism that Patriotism and anything that makes for love of Country, should be subject to attack whenever possible; the idea, of course, being to weaken such a spirit against the day of revolution." Mead concluded his article on the optimistic note that at least the public was becoming increasingly aware of the Communist threat: "This is a fight in which every person, who appreciates the liberty and freedom he now enjoys, under a democratic form of Government, must be interested, if Canada is to march forward and is to be allowed to work out her problems in peace and security."

This propaganda campaign continued throughout the 1930s.

In October 1935, the *Quarterly* carried an article entitled "Leninism" by Inspector R. Armitage, which dealt with the trial of the eight Communist leaders in Toronto in 1931 described elsewhere in this book, and reminded readers that Leninism was still just as big a menace as ever: "Although more than ten years have passed since Lenin's death his spirit endures, guiding the activities of his followers — members of his party — in Europe, Asia, America, Africa and Australia, bent on executing his plans for the establishment of a godless international Soviet Republic." In January 1936, an unsigned article in the *Quarterly* entitled "Training Young Communists" discussed Communist youth groups and the threat they represented to young Canadians.

The most extreme piece of right-wing propaganda to appear in the *RCMP Quarterly* during the 1930s was the reprint of "Peace, War and Communism," a paper delivered by Colonel C. E. Edgett before the Synod of the Presbyterian Church in Session at Vancouver, October 15, 1936. The editors of the *RCMP Quarterly* apparently considered the paper valuable enough to be brought to the attention of the rank-and-file members of the Force and the general public. Appearing in the issue of January 1937, Edgett's paper was not only anti-Communist and anti-Semitic, not only quick to accuse nearly everyone left of centre of being Communist sympathizers, but also openly sympathetic towards Fascist regimes in Europe.

A former chief of the Vancouver police force and penitentiary warden in New Westminster, Colonel Edgett began his speech to the assembled Presbyterians by lamenting the large number of pro-Communists in contemporary churches, particularly the United Church. "Moreover, Communism is the deadliest and most determined enemy of world peace — unless such peace be enforced under the iron rule of its own single world dictatorship." He warned every citizen who cherished peace to beware the "looming horrors of civil war caused by Communism."

After lambasting those "preachers, teachers and editors" of British Columbia who advocated "sympathy for the Reds," Edgett proceeded to describe world Communism as part of a Jewish conspiracy dating back to the eighteenth century, a main purpose of which was to destroy "all cherished feelings of patriotism or nationalism or race conscience." Just as Jewish Communists had allegedly infiltrated the Free Masons in the eighteenth century, so modern-day Communists "bored from within" churches, trade unions, political parties and other groups. Edgett portrayed the Democratic Party of the United States and about 400 major associations in North America as falling under the sway of international Communism due to the successful use of infiltration tactics.

Colonel Edgett then raised the subject of Fascism and criticized the General Council of the United Church for having recently denounced Fascism completely while allowing that there were some good things about Communism. He proceeded to declare himself in favour of the Fascist revolt in Spain and said he agreed with the sentiments of Cornelius Vanderbilt, whom he quoted from *Liberty* magazine: "Not only is this revolt from Bolshevism something new politically, but it is also the most saguinary religious war the centuries have seen."

Edgett then said that Fascism had some similarities to Communism in that both advocated power by violence and were opposed to democracy as practised in Canada.

> But there is this one essential difference. Communists are out to destroy nationhood and patriotism by ruthless violence — Fascists, or Nationalists, are out to preserve nationhood and patriotism by ruthless violence. There would have been no Fascism had there not first come Communism. And if Fascism had not arisen and conquered in Italy, and subsequently had not Nationalism arisen and conquered in Germany, then today those two great countries would have been obliterated from the map in a flood-tide of Bolshevism. The typical Fascist is not perfect by any means nor very admirable from the standpoint of the normal Democrat. But at least he has applied his violence and ferocity to the enemies of traditional family life — to the enemies of religion — and the Fascist states, as now established, are ruled neither by mere businessmen nor yet by fanatical revolutionaries.

These sentiments appeared in the *RCMP Quarterly* in January 1937; in less than three years Canada would be at war fighting those Fascist powers which the editor of the *RCMP Quarterly* appeared to admire in 1937. Edgett's arguments were, in fact, the type of arguments used by people who later became fifth columnists in France and other countries overrun by the Nazis after 1939. These people looked upon the world as becoming increasingly polarized between Fascism and

Communism and choose the former. Edgett ended his speech by calling upon national Communism:

The time has come in Canada for every person to stand forth and be counted as either for or against Communism. Tear the camouflage from the Red Beast — whether it be a religious camouflage or a trade union camouflage or a proletarian camouflage. Once the hideous form of the Beast is revealed for what it is, then I am confident that the great majority of Canadians will join in the national cause against it, and will declare for peace among themselves, instead of class-consciousness and class struggles and class-hatreds on which the Beast thrives!

After the outbreak of World War II in 1939, one of the duties of the RCMP was to arrest for internment members of Nazi and Fascist organizations in Canada. At first the Communist Party was also outlawed under the War Measures Act and its members interned, but after the Soviet Union entered the war in June 1941, many of the communists were released and entered the Canadian armed forces. One of the ironies of the war, then, was that it forced for a time at least the most outspoken RCMP officers to treat the extreme Right as enemies and the Communists as allies. And let it be said for them that even in these rather awkward circumstances they did their duty.

"Tools for Treachery" by Commissioner S. T. Wood appeared in the *RCMP Quarterly* of April 1941. In this article Wood described some of the new activities of the Force in combatting Canadian Nazis and Fascists since the outbreak of the war. He noted the increased work load of the Force which resulted from having to arrest or keep under observation supporters of Nazi, Fascist and Communist groups. Wood's list of groups allegedly constituting a danger to the state may well have alarmed civil libertarians and even caused some concern among the "law-and-order" crowd:

After these "Big Three" came a scattering of smaller subversive groups, such as The National Unity Party, the Technocrats, Jehovah's Witnesses and Youth Councils, some of which, like poison toadstool, sprang up over night to destroy out social structure. Not until Christianity and democracy had been mightily challenged did the people realize (and then but slowly) the strength, multiplicity and deadly malice of their foes.

The commissioner did not, of course, note the fact that many of the "foes" of 1941 had for the past two decades been looked upon by himself and his colleagues as allies in their struggle against Communism.

Wood devoted only about a third of his article to discussing RCMP actions directed against the far Right. The other two thirds he devoted to a favourite topic — the threat to Canadian society posed by Communists and those who would allow them normal civil rights:

Many may be surprised to hear that it is not the Nazi nor the Fascist but the radical who constitutes our most troublesome problem. Whereas the enemy alien is usually recognizable and easily rendered innocuous by clear-cut laws applicable to his case, your "Red" has the protection of citizenship, his foreign master is not officially an enemy and, unless he blunders into the open and provides proof of his guilt, he is much more difficult to suppress. Since Communism was outlawed, most of his work is carried on under cover of other organizations and associations, pretending to be, or in reality, loyal to the Constitution.

He warned of the Communist tactics of infiltrating trade unions, youth groups and other associations, and in so doing revealed his outlook towards some of Canada's less fortunate citizens:

The Communists, always quick to take advantage of human misery in any form, found the unemployed and underpaid easy tools for the spread of their doctrines of hatred. The criminal and weakminded classes were even more dazzled by their promises of gain.

Wood's main attack, in fact, focussed not on the Communists themselves but on the "tools of treachery" allegedly manipulated by the secret conspiracy. He paid special attention to trade unionists and civil rights associations who he felt furthered the aims of Communism by demanding political rights for Communists.

Commissioner Wood cut a wide swath when he identified Canada's "tools for treachery." He even included portions of the press and Parliament.

Whenever possible the Communist takes advantage of the public press to aid grievances. On several occasions he has succeeded in gaining the editorial ear as a martyr to religious and political intolerance and has thus temporarily embarrassed a conscientious Government. Fortunately, the great majority of editors place country above party in such times as this, affording a splendid guarantee of good government and the perpetuation of democratic principles, and only through deception can they be so used. For instance it was largely due to lack of facts that some papers severely arraigned the Government for interning "labour leaders" when these were in reality Communist leaders; for persecuting religion in the guise of Jehovah's Witnesses when, in truth, these are active enemies of Christianity and democracy; for employing Gestapo methods through the Police in investigating and seizing "harmless citizens", when the Police had ample evidence that these citizens were plotting against the State. The intermittent attacks on the Defence of Canada Regulations is almost entirely due to lack of understanding, taken advantage of by extremists and pacifists, who are well aware that it is the Regulations alone that prevent them from accomplishing their anti-British designs.

Wood went further and implied that *any* criticism of government war policies, particularly of the Defence of Canada Regulations, was playing into the hands of the Communists:

Communists are quick to glean comfort from public men and women who criticize Government war policies. A few parliamentarians, who are apparently sincere but obviously uninformed or indifferent to facts, are greatly encouraging the subversive elements by attacking the Defence Regulations.

What the commissioner was demanding was a completely free hand for the government and the RCMP to deny people civil rights under the War Measures Act. He expected people to give their allegiance to the government unconditionally and their trust to a supposedly benevolent dictatorship for the duration of the war. The idea that the Defence of Canada Regulations under the War Measures Act might be abused was not even considered. The act was, of course, grossly abused during World War II as it had been during World War I and would be again during the "October Crisis" in Quebec in 1970.

Some Communists remained interned long after the Soviet Union had entered the war and most Canadian Communists able to do so had taken up arms on behalf of the Allied cause. The most infamous injustice perpetrated under the auspices of the War Measures Act was the internment of Japanese Canadians in British Columbia. Their property was confiscated and they were moved from coastal areas to internment camps in interior British Columbia on the alleged grounds that they *might* be used as spies and saboteurs for Japan. The compensation they received for confiscated property was a tiny fraction of its actual value. Other reasons for their removal have since come to light, such as sheer racial prejudice and the desire to eliminate the Japanese Canadians from competition in the fishing and market gardening industries. To this day Canada has done nothing significant to compensate the Japanese Canadians for the injustices they suffered during World War II.

Judging from their political opinions, Commissioner Wood and his colleagues took action against Nazis and Fascists not because they were vehemently opposed to their philosophy but because they could be used as agents of enemy powers during wartime. RCMP officials did not put emphasis on refuting the basic tenets of National Socialism and Fascism or on a propaganda campaign against them, though they did occasionally refer to people supporting these movements as "poisonous toadstools" and agents of enemy countries. According to liberal theorists this would be quite proper because the police in a liberal democracy are not supposed to be involved in political debate and should confine themselves to carrying out the lawful orders of the duly elected government of the day. However, it must be pointed out that although the RCMP stuck fairly close to this role in their dealings with the Right during World War II, they did not do so nor had they ever done so in the past with respect to the Left. The RCMP and many other government officials abused the powers conferred on them by the War Measures Act to settle old scores with the Left and to pander to popular prejudice by moving against minority racial groups such as Canadians of Japanese ancestry. The campaign against the Left subsided after 1941 because of the political exigencies of the alliance with the Soviet Union, but it was renewed with even greater vigour as the Cold War developed in the late 1940s.

Chapter 7
The RCMP and the Cold War

In Fulton, Missouri, in March, 1946, Winston Churchill delivered the speech which many people take to be the signal for the inauguration of the Cold War. A few weeks prior to Churchill's speech, the Cold War had already begun in Canada, accompanied by sensational stories revolving around the defection of Igor Gouzenko from the Soviet embassy the previous September. Gouzenko had taken documents with him which purported to show that a Soviet spy ring involving Canadian citizens and Soviet diplomatic officials was operating in Canada. The investigations and trials that followed these revelations by the government in February 1946 were to help set the tone of the political atmosphere in Canada during the late 1940s. Some information had been illegally supplied to the U.S.S.R., but the way the case was handled went far beyond any normal apprehension and conviction of spies. It was blown up to gigantic proportions throughout the Western world as part of what might be termed the "initiation ceremonies" for the years of Cold War which were to follow. William A. Reuben describes in *The Atom Spy Hoax* the official reaction to the Gouzenko revelations as calculated to destroy any pro-Soviet feeling that had carried over from the wartime alliance and to initiate a thrust to the right in North American politics. This was politically necessary if the Western nations were to embark upon the so-called "containment" strategy later exemplified by the formation of NATO and the Korean War and further developed and articulated by John Foster Dulles during the 1950s.

The methods of procedure adopted by the government in the wake of the Gouzenko revelations indicated that the authorities were not going to be squeamish about the violation of civil liberties in the post-war era. On February 5, 1946, more than a week before anything was known by the public, four members of the Cabinet passed a secret order-in-council under the War Measures Act, appointing a Royal Commission and giving it sweeping authority to disregard normal legal safeguards in detaining for questioning anyone who, in the judgement of the minister of justice or the prime minister, was believed to be "acting in any manner prejudicial to the public safety or the safety of the State."[1] Under these regulations, the RCMP were given a blank cheque of the type used to intern people during both world wars. B. K. Sandwell, editor of *Saturday Night*, described some of the results in an article which appeared in the American liberal journal *The Nation* on May 4, 1946.

> ... Thirteen persons were seized and detained by plainclothes officers of the Royal Canadian Mounted Police, rushed to the RCMP barracks in an Ottawa suburb, and held there, with no charge made against them and with no opportunity to communicate with counsel, for periods ranging from two and a half to six weeks . . .
>
> For two and a half weeks after February 15 none of the thirteen persons were allowed to see even their nearest relatives. For the first ten days the only communication allowed was between husbands and wives by censored mail. It was not until twelve days after the seizure that the secret order-in-council was published, and until that time it was impossible for lawyers engaged by relatives, to learn by what authority the detained persons were being held.[2]

The Official Secrets Act, passed in 1939, determined the procedures adopted by the Royal Commission in its investigation. The Royal Commission declared in its final report that the act shifts "the burden of proof from the State to the accused, and in such cases it is for the person, against whom an offence under the statute is alleged, to establish his innocence to the reasonable satisfaction of the tribunal charged with the responsibility of deciding."[3] Certain sections of the act were so sweeping that they could be used to imprison almost anyone who had been on reasonably friendly terms with someone suspected of being the agent of a foreign power. The act also had some similarities to statutes like Section 98 of the Criminal Code in that the burden of proof was on the accused rather than the Crown. Perhaps the most dangerous sections of the act included the following:

> Section 3 (2) On a prosecution under this section, it shall not be necessary to show that the accused person was guilty of any particular act tending to show a purpose prejudicial to the safety or interests of the State, and, notwithstanding

that no such act is proved against him, he may be convicted. . .

(3) In any proceedings against a person for an offence under this section, the fact that he has been in communication with, or attempted to communicate with, an agent of a foreign power whether within or without Canada, shall be evidence that he has for a purpose prejudicial to the safety or interests of the State, obtained or attempted to obtain information which is calculated to be or might be or is intended to be directly or indirectly useful to a foreign power.

Section 4. A person shall, unless he proves to the contrary, be deemed to have been in communication with an agent of a foreign power if he has, either within or without Canada . . . visited the address of an agent of a foreign power or consorted or associated with such agent. . .

The expression "an agent of a foreign power" includes any person who is or has been or is reasonably suspected of being or having been employed by a foreign power either within or without Canada, prejudicial to the safety or interests of the State. . . ."[4]

Just in case the provisions of the Official Secrets Act were not sufficiently encompassing, the government's order-in-council empowered the Royal Commissioners to force witnesses to give evidence, and this was interpreted to mean that people could be required to testify against themselves even though the testimony would be used against them in court at a later period. The Royal Commission openly admitted in their report that they denied people the right to consult lawyers during their investigations. "We considered it expedient in the exercise of the discretion given us by the statute not to accede immediately to the request of a witness for representation."[5] Several of the accused were, in fact, held incommunicado and questioned for weeks, and some were left convicted on the basis of this testimony. The Royal Commission, after employing the tactics described above, publicly named 20 people as having been spies. Of these, ten were convicted and sentenced, nine were acquitted and one was never tried. As Reuben points out, it is a wonder any were acquitted in the light of the procedures adopted.

These procedures in the cases following from the Gouzenko defection evoked widespread criticism from individuals and associations concerned with civil liberties and from some sections of the daily press and other media. There was also considerable debate in Parliament, and members of all parties offered criticisms of government tactics. A Conservative M.P., A. L. Smith, declared, "The people of this country will always regret and will never live down the fact that we threw aside and abrogated the rights and liberties of our citizens."[6] These criticisms were, however, drowned out by the hysteria whipped up by government leaders, who fostered the misconception that "atomic secrets" had been sold to the Russians and that Canada was thereby threatened by Communist infiltration.

It was not until years later that it became respectable to view the events of 1946 in a reasonably objective manner. In an article in *Maclean's* March 15, 1954, Blair Fraser put the whole affair into more realistic perspective:

> The spies that Igor Gouzenko exposed, far from being eminent and uniquely trusted, were little people of no great account. Much of the information that they gave to the Russians was trivial but the Canadian Government did not fail to take the conspiracy seriously. Once it was convinced that Igor Gouzenko was telling the truth it acted with unprecedented harshness.
>
> More than a dozen suspects were got out of bed before dawn and held incommunicado, with no charge laid against them, for weeks while they were examined without benefit of counsel. Some who were later convicted of espionage were convicted largely on their own testimony, given before the Royal Commission. Some who refused to talk were acquitted; the Crown had no admissable evidence against them.[7]

Fraser went on to point out that such flagrant violation of civil liberties could not have happened in the United States, where individuals were given more protection by the Bill of Rights, but that certain varieties of witch-hunting were more serious in that country than in Canada.

The broader implications of the atmosphere created by the spy sensations of 1946 and other Cold War events were to affect far more people than those suspected of having committed espionage. The political psychology which would lead to McCarthyism in the United States and to a much milder version of it in Canada was beginning to take shape. The outbreak of the Korean War in 1950 made the situation even worse. In Canada this atmosphere was exemplified by an obsession with internal security, which led to the dismissal or forced resignation of scores of people from government departments and agencies on the grounds that they were security risks or *might become* security risks. Many more were either demoted or denied promotions.

Government departments adopted a policy of requiring employees and applicants for employment to undergo security checks for a wide variety of jobs which should not have required security clearance at all. People were sometimes even forced to resign from their jobs on the grounds that they *might* be security risks. One such instance was that of Stanley Rands, an employee of the National Film Board, now a professor of psychology at the University of Saskatchewan Regina Campus. Rands, who belonged to nothing more radical than a civil liberties committee and the Civil Service Association, was told by his superior, "We know you are not a Communist, but the point is that some people think you are." Following his resignation from the Film Board, Rands was hired as assistant director of health education in the Saskatchewan Department of Health but the RCMP apparently tried to deprive him of that job as well. He was told by the director of administration that the RCMP had called to make enquiries about him. Fortunately for Rands the Saskatchewan CCF government at that time was not as fearful as the federal government and the enquiry did not bring about a second dismissal. However, it was a typical RCMP practice, which undoubtedly cost scores of people their employment and denied promotion to others.

Investigations for security clearance purposes were carried out by the Security and Intelligence branch of the RCMP and, given their political outlook, one can well imagine some of the facts they would consider relevant. The people being investigated did not have to be, and hardly ever were, informed of the fact; nor were they entitled to see their dossiers or to hear any of the evidence that might be used against them. Much of the information in the dossiers was based on hearsay, rumours and interrogation of neighbours and acquaintances, often dealing with associations and events from years back. The S & I branch fully investigated thousands of people during the years.[8]

The typical procedure in government departments was for the security committee or individual in charge to appraise the RCMP reports and then decide the fate of the employee or employees in question. There was no appeal to any outside authority, and it sometimes happened that the person concerned would be denied promotion, demoted or fired without any explanation.[9] Departments preferred to get rid of people quietly and without publicity; government spokesmen even argued that this was more humane because in view of the political atmosphere of the time it made it easier for the victims to secure employment in the private sector of the economy. While some people might argue that this secrecy was preferable to the public witch-hunts going on in the United States, they would have to admit that it denied people the elementary right of defending themselves and allowed the dirty work to continue free of criticism from Parliament or the press.

Because of the secret methods of operation, only a small fraction of the injustices perpetrated upon individuals ever came to public attention. Some which did were anything but flattering to the government and particularly to the RCMP. One such case, revealed by Sidney Katz in an article in *Maclean's* in 1963, involved a 27-year-old man who was discharged from the RCAF for no apparent reason in 1952.[10] After losing several more jobs, the man took his case to T.C. Douglas, then premier of Saskatchewan, who interceded on his behalf with the federal minister of justice and the commissioner of the RCMP. The commissioner informed Douglas that at one time the man had been secretary of a Communist youth organization in Regina. Upon further investigation by Douglas, it turned out that the man had never been a Communist but had once been secretary of a CCF Youth organization. One of his former schoolteachers had facetiously referred to him as "a young Bolshevik" to an RCMP investigator, and this had been duly kept in his record for years as part of the evidence against him. The incompetence of the RCMP in this case is almost as depressing as their high-handedness.

One did not have to work for the government to come under RCMP surveillance. Any company with a contract to undertake classified defence work for the government had to send to Ottawa a list of all employees who might be given access to classified information. These people were then investigated without their knowledge by the RCMP and the findings sent to the Defence Production Department. This department would then decide which employees were "security risks" and send a list to the company concerned. When they were criticized for this procedure, the government insisted that they did not wish to threaten people's livelihood but only to ensure that "security risks" did not gain access to classified information. However, employers sometimes took it upon themselves to fire people who had been identified as "security risks," presumably on the grounds that they did not want to employ "Reds". One such case, brought to light by a Conservative M.P., concerned G. Robert Jackson, who was fired by A. V. Roe Company, aircraft manufacturers, and could not discover why. It turned out that after being surreptitiously investigated by the RCMP, Jackson had been designated a security risk and fired forthwith. Jackson's was one of the few cases which became a public scandal. It was publicized by the press and the authorities were criticized for it in such respectable media as *Maclean's,* all of which may have helped to make the authorities after that somewhat less callous about trampling people underfoot.[11]

During the Cold War the RCMP did not confine themselves to investigating people who worked for the government or for companies holding defence contracts. The RCMP investigated anyone in the country who they thought *might be or might become* a "danger to the State." This sometimes involved not only investigating but also harassing people. The harassment of Communists and their associates has been discussed in Chapter 4 on the S & I branch of the Force. Sidney Katz has related a couple of the more absurd examples of harassment to illustrate how broadly at least some agents of the S & I defined subversion.[12] One was the case of a Winnipeg high school student who wrote a satirical letter of a slightly radical nature to one of the local daily newspapers. He suggested that Santa Claus was a Communist because he gave away free gifts. Two S & I agents visited the boy in his school, questioned him on his political beliefs, and warned him that if he did not stick to more orthodox views they would see to it that he never obtained a job of any consequence. Another case, which T. C. Douglas raised in the House of Commons, concerned a 74-year-old Regina widow who described herself as a Christian pacifist by persuasion. She was visited occasionally for 20 years by an S & I officer who questioned her about her political beliefs and associations. On one such visit the officer asked her, among other things, about the alleged Communist affiliations of the Hon. I. C. (Toby) Nollet, a Saskatchewan cabinet minister, who had been a friend of her late husband.

It is to Canada's credit that, despite the many unsavory

aspects of official policy during the 1950s, Red-baiting and witch-hunting did not reach the hysterical proportions they did in the United States. We had our witch-hunters, to be sure, but none of the horrifying stature of Senator Joseph McCarthy. Perhaps the most notorious politician of the McCarthy type of Canada was Reverend Blackmore, a Social Credit M.P. from Alberta who attempted to improve on the theory of the "international Jewish Communist conspiracy" by throwing in the "financiers" and the "Mongolians" for good measure. Fortunately, few people took him seriously. The official publications of the RCMP during these years, however, espoused a right-wing philosophy perfectly compatible with Reverend Blackmore's, and which must have rivalled that of the FBI at its most fearsome.

One of the ideological contributions of the RCMP to the Cold War was a book entitled *Law and Order in Canadian Democracy*. The first edition appeared in 1949 with an introduction by Commissioner S. T. Wood, and a revised edition, introduced by Commissioner L. H. Nicholson, came out in 1952. The book contained a series of lectures by RCMP officers, revised and edited for publication by a committee chaired by Lt. Col. The Honourable Wilfrid Bovey, chairman of the International Relations Committee, International Association of Chiefs of Police.

The lectures contained in *Law and Order in Canadian Democracy* covered a variety of criminal topics of interest to the police and the public, including organized crime, narcotics, counterfeiting, etc. There were also lectures of a more explicitly political nature on treason, sedition, Communism, public disturbances, Fascism, law and democracy, etc. The emphasis on political crimes is considerable, and in the Foreward to the 1952 edition Lt. Col. Bovey reveals what was probably one of the main reasons for publishing the book:

Freedom is our most precious possession. For the sake of freedom, since 1914, the people of Canada with other peoples of the Commonwealth, the United States and allies have fought two terrible wars. With same allies, in 1950 Canadians entered the struggle for Korea. For the sake of freedom, to guard against the ever-growing danger of a tyranny such as the world has never known, Canada signed the North Atlantic Treaty.

Not only from without is freedom threatened, it is threatened from within. We are no longer complacent towards threats from without but we must avoid complacency in the face of threats from within. The most serious threat of all comes from those who use their liberty to enjoy license, whose anti-social works endanger the foundations of democracy.[13]

In case the message did not get across, it is repeated in the second paragraph of Chapter I:

Undermining and subversive influences in Canada today thrive on ignorance and lack of appreciation of the full meaning of true democracy. A well-informed public can throw off and smash the hold of subversive ideologies. And it is the absolute duty of every Canadian citizen to become well-informed, and thus bring to light and destroy the ugly cancer which at this very moment is gnawing at the vitals of democracy.[14]

The subversive ideologies "gnawing at the vitals of democracy" are explained more fully in the chapters entitled "Fascism and National Socialism" and "Communism." The attitude towards Fascism and National Socialism is particularly interesting. It is not surprising that the RCMP were critical of these philosophies in view of the fact that World War II and the horrors revealed at the Nuremberg trials were still fresh in people's minds. The criticism of National Socialism in the book, however, is tinged with regret that the excesses of Hitler and other leaders had made this system unacceptable:

National Socialism could probably have been made to work in Germany if its leadership had not fallen into the hands of demagogues and sadists whose excesses were to bring death or ruin to millions of people. It need hardly be emphasized how advantageous it would have been if Germany had found a system suited to the idiosyncrasies of her people, a system by which she could have grown strong and prosperous and become a bulwark against the encroachment of Communism.[15]

The RCMP were, however, at least officially, opposed to Fascism as an ideology, a position very different from the one they took in the 1930s. "To those who are doubtful of democracy's ability to solve its own social and economic problems and who think that Fascism is the antidote to Communism, a little reflection on the brutalities which accompanied the forcing of that regime on the people of Italy and Germany should be salutary."[16] No one, of course, recommended a little reflection on public espousals by RCMP officials during the late 1930s.

The opinions on Communism expressed in *Law and Order in Canadian Democracy* were merely an updating of the propaganda campaign the authorities and the RCMP had been carrying on intermittently since World War I. They again warned people that Communists and their "fellow travellers" lurked in trade unions, peace movements, civil liberties associations and other groups and that, while they might sometimes employ "Trojan horse tactics" as opposed to open confrontation, their aim remained that of establishing a terroristic dictatorship dedicated to destroying anything that resembled human decency. "No matter what may be its coat — and it has had many colours in the last 27 years — underneath there still beats the black heart of dictatorship, the spirit which is essentially traitorous and anti-democratic."[17] They also warned that Communists would be a continuous problem because of their fanticism and perseverance:

A convinced Communist is a man possessed. He is not amenable to argument or persuasion, or even coercion. Society must always be on guard against him, and each citizen must be prepared to combat his ideas wherever they crop up.[18]

Throughout the 1950s, references to Communism as a serious threat to Canadian society appeared periodically in RCMP publications and in the speeches of high-ranking officers of the Force. They even continued into the 1960s, after the Cold War jitters had generally receded and the Canadian Communist Party itself had declined in numbers and strength almost to the point of irrelevance. Nevertheless, disrespect for the police and authority in general continued to be viewed as a part of the everlasting Communist conspiracy, played out consciously by "Reds" or unconsciously by the "tools for treachery." Speaking to the conference of the Canadian Association of Chiefs of Police in 1961, George McClellan, deputy commissioner of the RCMP, claimed that there was more antipathy to authority in Canada than ever before and warned that a disrespect for authority and a lack of discipline had always appeared in the past "when civilization was on the way down the drain."[19]

Speaking to the International Association of Chiefs of Police in Montreal the same year, Commissioner C. W. Harvison bemoaned increasing public antagonism to the police around the world and listed "Communist propaganda" as one of the causes. Harvison warned that the Communists could be winning the propaganda war with the West and cited this as the most important reason for renewed efforts at stamping out crime in Western countries.

> There is an urgency even beyond that of protecting citizens from criminality. Our increasing crime rate is an ugly blot that must be erased. Until that has been done, the blot can be and is being used in the cold war as an indication of the weakness of democracy. In fact until this blot has been removed it does demonstrate a weakness.[20]

It never occurred to Harvison to point a finger at the social conditions that cause "criminality" or at the politicians who tolerated and even co-operated with organized crime. Nor did he mention the fact that the RCMP had co-operated with Hal Banks, one of Canada's more notorious criminals, apparently on the assumption shared by the politicians and employers that criminals of the conventional type were less of a threat to the status quo than Communists. (Banks had been brought into Canada from the United States with the connivance of the Canadian government and the RCMP to run the Seafarers' International Union (SIU) and smash the Canadian Seamen's Union (CSU), which was led by Communists. Legally Banks should have been barred from the country because of his criminal record. He succeeded in destroying the CSU but established such a reign of terror on the Great Lakes that eventually the government had to move against him and the SIU, which they themselves helped to create. The government's move against Banks and the SIU did not occur, however, until the 1960s.) Harvison might also have noted that at the time he was speaking about 500 of approximately 8,500 members of the RCMP were employed by the S & I branch of the Force. Perhaps some of the personnel engaged in harassing widows and high school students might have been better employed investigating the connections between organized crime and politicians.

The opinions of police officials in Canada on law and order

and political protest did not differ basically from their American counterparts. One gets the impression that RCMP officials admired J. Edgar Hoover and would have liked to speak out as frequently and as vociferously as he did, but that they did not dare to. Hoover's ideas on the main problems facing police forces in the United States were expressed in a speech to the International Association of Chiefs of Police in 1960, quoted in the *RCMP Quarterly* in January 1961. "As members of a profession dedicated to preserving America's God-given heritage of equality and justice for all, law enforcement has been subjected to relentless attack by the Communists, the hatemongers, the pseudo-liberals and others who would destroy the very foundations of this great Republic."[21] Hoover then went on to denounce youth, labour and disarmament groups and, as usual, claimed that nearly all anti-Establishment activity was directed by the Communist Party, which "remains an inseparable arm of the treacherous atheistic international conspiracy which is being directed against the free world from Moscow."[22]

In the early 1960s the RCMP, like their counterparts in the United States, were somewhat out of date in their conception of the groups likely to be involved in fomenting demonstrations against the government and in mounting attacks on the status quo generally. The RCMP went right on insisting that the small and generally passive Communist Party in Canada represented the great threat. Soon, however, they were to realize their mistake and begin increasing their surveillance and harassment of peace movements, New Left student groups, Quebec separatists, American draft dodgers, dissident professors, discontented farmers and any others they found organizing against the prevailing political and economic system.

Chapter 8
The 1960s: Students, draft dodgers and farmers

The RCMP continued to harass members of the Communist Party and affiliated organizations throughout the 1960s, despite the fact that the party and its activities were perfectly legal. In its tactics (as distinct from its philosophy) the Communist Party had become, in fact, similar to other parties though not so successful, in that much of its emphasis was on disseminating propaganda and contesting elections. Nevertheless the RCMP continued with its infiltration and surveillance of the Communist Party and of numerous "front groups" and trade unions in which Communists were active. Instructions to S & I agents in 1960 listed 30 Communists organizations and "front groups" in addition to five trade unions deemed subversive that threatened democracy and should be watched closely. RCMP instructions described the aims and objectives of these groups in some detail, presumably to make security agents aware of just how dangerous they were. One group listed was the Canadian Chinese Friendship Society, whose aims and objectives were described as follows:

> Its primary function is to pressure the Canadian government to obtain diplomatic recognition of China and campaign for closer cultural and economic ties with Communist China. In addition to local celebrations in support of Communist China, the C.C.F.S. has sponsored delegations to China which, on return, have afforded this organization an opportunity to capitalize on pro-Chinese propaganda.

Obviously, such aims could scarcely be described as revolutionary; and in this case it is clear that Communists and their sympathizers were harassed and followed about not because they were involved in any secret conspiracy to overthrow the government but because they were defined by the RCMP and their political superiors as representatives of an alien and evil philosophy. The Force instructs its agents that:

> Every Communist is a dedicated revolutionist and pledged

to the destruction of our political and economic freedom. Communism is subversive because it preaches the overturn of our form of government by force, it is tyrannical because it stands for the destruction of political freedom, it is treacherous because it compels obedience to a "Party line" formulated outside this country, rather than to a duly constituted authority. Communism is a highly organized world movement opposed to true democracy and to the freedom of the individual.

It follows from this definition that the police, as the supposed representatives of society as a whole should not only keep a close eye on Communists but also be seen to be doing so. Members of the public would then be discouraged from having anything to do with Communists lest they, too, come under surveillance. And so through the 1960s the RCMP followed prominent Communists wherever they went.

In some cases the situation reached the point of absurdity. Nigel Morgan, party leader in British Columbia, was dubbed by his colleagues "Two-Car Morgan" after being followed by two RCMP cars throughout a 7,000-mile tour of the province.[1] Occasionally there were advantages to close surveillance in that one had help close at hand in the event of an accident. Bill Beeching, a long-time leader of the Communist Party in Saskatchewan, related how on his way to Saskatoon for a May Day meeting in 1969 he overturned his car near Davidson, Saskatchewan. He was thrown from the car and unable to get up. Minutes later the undercover agent who had been following him arrived on the scene and announced that he had already radioed for an ambulance. He then made Beeching comfortable and chided him for his driving while they waited for the arrival of the ambulance. "Whatever happened to you? I always put you down as a good driver." Despite such assistance in the rare accident, tailing as a rule was of course a political liability.

The Security and Intelligence branch began extending its activities considerably during the early 1960s, as the peace movement gained strength and the political psychology connected with the Cold War gradually declined. In Canada the peace movement was led by such groups as the Campaign for Nuclear Disarmament (CND) and the Combined Universities Campaign for Nuclear Disarmament (CUCND), which adopted many of their ideas from the peace movement lead by

Bertrand Russell in Great Britain. The main objective of the movement in this country was to prevent Canada from acquiring nuclear weapons. The main activists in the nuclear disarmament movement were on the university campuses, but they enjoyed considerable support from the public at large. The campaign against acquisition of nuclear weapons was supported by highly respectable, non-partisan groups such as the Voice of Women, in which Maryon Pearson, wife of the late Prime Minister Lester B. Pearson, played a role at one time. At different times during the 1960s, opposition to Canadian acquisition of nuclear weapons was even adopted as party policy by the New Democratic, Liberal and Progressive Conservative parties.

Despite its moderate policies and respectable adherents, the peace movement was always considered a subversive threat by right-wing pro-American political circles and by the RCMP. Members of the movement were extremely critical of American foreign policy and Canadian subservience to that policy. They organized mass protest demonstrations and sometimes resorted to the type of civil disobedience tactics common to Bertrand Russell's peace movement in Britain and the civil rights campaigns led by Martin Luther King in the United States. Young people who joined the peace movement because of their opposition to nuclear weapons often developed a critical attitude towards many other aspects of Western society as well. These developments were anathema to the authoritarian directors of the RCMP.

The reaction of the RCMP to this new ferment was to increase the activities of the S & I branch of the Force. They began recruiting spies on university campuses and within organizations such as CUCND. By 1962 many people were expressing alarm at the excessive amount of spying and harassment that was going on. Due to the clumsiness and incompetence of some S & I officers, people could not help knowing about these activities. In one case, at Laval University, the RCMP attempted to spy on the editors of the student newspaper *Le Carabin*, because they supported the nuclear disarmament movement. An RCMP officer approached Jacqueline Cyr and asked her to spy on Helen Sénècal and Edward Smith, two of the editors in question. Jacqueline Cyr refused to co-operate and blew the whistle on the RCMP, who admitted to the accusation but did not apologize for it. One RCMP officer was quoted as saying, "Next time, we'll try and find someone more reliable than Cyr."[2]

Other cases came to the public's attention in 1962 and 1963. One case, raised by T. C. Douglas in the House of Commons, concerned a nuclear disarmament demonstration organized by CUCND in front of the Saskatchewan Legislature on April 1, 1961.[3] The RCMP took pictures and names of several of the demonstrators and later visited their homes for the purpose of harassing them about their political activities. An RCMP officer visited the father of one of these demonstrators in Yorkton, Saskatchewan, and warned him that his son could get into trouble if he did not dissociate himself from the peace movement. Another case involved Lionel Orlikow, a Winnipeg high school teacher and brother of David Orlikow, M.P. While conducting visiting American students on a tour of Winnipeg, Orlikow had stopped, among other places, at the headquarters of the Communist Party. When he was afterwards interrogated by the RCMP, his brother raised the matter in the House of Commons. Another case concerned a theology student who revealed to journalist Sidney Katz that he had been a part-time secret agent for the RCMP with CUCND for about a year.

Many incidents of this kind were brought to public attention by opposition M.P.'s in the House of Commons during 1962 and 1963. Several more were revealed by Sidney Katz in an article entitled "Inside Canada's Secret Police," which appeared in the April 20, 1963, issue of *Maclean's*. RCMP harassment had in fact become so obnoxious in some quarters that people were beginning to object strenuously. The Canadian Association of University Teachers (CAUT), alarmed at the RCMP threat to academic freedom on the university campuses, proposed the following resolution at their council meeting of June 1962:

> Resolved, that the Canadian Association of University Teachers express its disapproval of questions concerning the political or religious beliefs, activities or associations of students or colleagues. Members of the Association are advised not to answer such questions, even when they are part of the security investigation of persons seeking government employment.[5]

This resolution was then distributed to local associations throughout the country for discussion, and a statement accompanying it in the *CAUT Bulletin* indicated that the principal of one university had already objected publicly to RCMP activities on the campuses and that the Force had come under fire from newspapers and M.P.'s. As of November 1962, the federal government had neither denied that such spying was taking place nor disavowed the practice. When CAUT efforts to gain assurances from the Department of Justice that RCMP activities would not be allowed to threaten academic freedom brought no response, the CAUT Council passed an expanded version of their proposed resolution of June 1962. A similar resolution was passed by the National Federation of Canadian University Students (NFCUS), and complaints were registered by the Voice of Women and other organizations which had been subjected to RCMP surveillance. These developments plus constant questioning by a few members of Parliament led to a controversy which went on for well over a year before the federal authorities agreed to a limited curtailment of RCMP activities on university campuses and in some other areas.

The way two different governments — the Diefenbaker government and the Pearson government which replaced it in 1963 — handled the controversy over campus activities revealed both dishonesty and a callous attitude toward civil liberties on the part of many politicians. The first response of government officials to criticisms of RCMP questioning and surveillance was to deny that such activities were taking place. On several occasions the minister of justice and his officials made statements which were untrue — either deliberately or because they had been misinformed by RCMP officials.[6] When T. C. Douglas first raised the question of the Yorkton youth whose father had been interviewed by the RCMP, then Justice Minister Davie Fulton publicly denied that any such interview had taken place. Fulton later admitted in a letter to the attorney-general of Saskatchewan that such an interview had indeed, taken place, but he never issued a correction of his former public statement.[7] Under questioning in the House of Commons on December 14, 1962, Minister of Justice Donald Fleming claimed that only people requiring security clearance for public employment were investigated by the RCMP on campuses. "I am told, Mr. Chairman, that there is no special security activities in relation to students carried on by the RCMP, and that the police have not been approaching persons in universities with a view to developing sources of information."[8] This was after the Laval incident involving Jacqueline

Cyr and after the CAUT and the principal of at least one university had complained about such investigations. On January 21, 1963, T. M. Bell, parliamentary secretary to the minister of justice, said, "Members of the RCMP are not engaged in interviewing students and faculty members at Canadian universities about the political views and political activities of other faculty members."[9] One month later, on February 22, Rev. J. W. E. Newberry, principal of Huntington College at Sudbury, was being questioned by Inspector Wiebe of the RCMP about the political opinions of his staff and students.[10]

In a press interview on March 21, 1963, RCMP Commissioner C. W. Harvison let the cat out of the bag by admitting that it was the regular policy of the Force to investigate suspected political activity on university campuses.[11] Harvison also insinuated that police surveillance was necessary to keep students from going astray.

> University students are naturally curious. At this age one finds a great deal of idealism and a strong sence of social morality. There are certain abuses in our system which the student may think communism will cure, if he gets only one side of the picture.[12]

Harvison added: "It is only those who have made a careful study of this problem, such as the various security services, that can differentiate between the radical or dissenter and the conspirator."[13] The Commissioner dismissed any criticisms of the RCMP as being Communist inspired or perhaps even part of a conscious conspiracy. He cited as evidence the fact that William Kashtan, a prominent leader of the Communist Party of Canada, had addressed an international Communist conference in Prague the previous summer on how to fight anti-communism. "It was only a short time after his return that we began to see increased criticism aimed at the RCMP."[14]

The Pearson government, which replaced the Diefenbaker government in the spring of 1963, proved to be little different from its predecessor when it came to defending the political activities of the RCMP. Under questioning in the House of Commons on June 3, 1963, Minister of Justice Lionel Chevrier cited the alleged Communist menace as reason enough for the RCMP activities. "It is an avowed objective of the Communists in Canada to infiltrate universities, to infiltrate a number of other organizations whose purposes, though proper, they could subvert to their own ends."[15] Chevrier went on to claim that some faculty members favoured RCMP investigations on campuses and that the Force was supported by a majority of the country's press. He also declared that a parliamentary committee of enquiry would be out of the question because it might reveal S & I procedures to the enemy. He criticized Sidney Katz for having had the audacity to publish his exposé in *Maclean's* without allowing Commissioner Harvison to view the contents in advance.

Chevrier's responses on June 3 were typical of the attitude of the Department of Justice throughout the spring of 1963, and seemed to prove the accuracy of charges made by David Orlikow a few days previously! "It seems to me from reading old *Hansards* that the more ministers of justice change the more they are the same, because as they change and take their portfolios they seem to be very well briefed by the RCMP, so that whatever the RCMP does becomes right and proper."[16]

On July 31, 1963, two CAUT representatives, Professors Bora Laskin and J. H. Stewart Reid, met with Prime Minister Pearson, Justice Minister Chevrier, Pauline Jewett, M.P., and Gordon Robertson, clerk of the Privy Council, to discuss the problem of RCMP surveillance on the campuses. They also advised the CAUT representatives that a re-examination of policy and procedures regarding security was under way and that the committee in charge would, among other things, be examining the way such procedures applied to university campuses. In their report to the CAUT membership, Laskin and Reid indicated that the government's response to their concerns had been mixed.

> No clear response was made to our expression of concern about general "watch-dog" surveillance unrelated to investigation of a specific person needing security clearance to occupy a particular post. Lastly it was our impression that this Government intends to see that the RCMP desists from policy declarations, and as far as possible from public utterances on contentious questions.[18]

The impression that the government intended to prevent the RCMP from making public statements on contentious questions turned out to be fairly accurate, but the ban was perhaps a mixed blessing. For while the police commenting on political questions may have been out of keeping, at least they allowed the victims of the police to see what sort of obscurantist mentality they were up against.

By the autumn of 1963 the government began making gestures towards reforming the security system by giving those public servants subject to security checks a few rights and by agreeing to curtail some of the wholesale surveillance about which people outside the public service were complaining. On October 25 Prime Minister Pearson announced to the House of Commons that the government was establishing a board of review to examine cases where public servants had been recommended for dismissal for security reasons. The board would make its views known in such cases, and the appropriate ministers would then decide whether to recommend dismissal to Cabinet. The prime minister stated on October 29, that the new procedures had no bearing on RCMP surveillance of campuses and that the government would soon be meeting with university representatives on that question.

During November 1963, representatives of the government and the commissioner of the RCMP met with CAUT representatives and members of NFCUS. On December 4 Jack Davis, parliamentary secretary to Prime Minister Pearson, in answer to a question from Stanley Knowles, assured the House that there would be no investigations on campuses except in cases where individuals either had applied for jobs requiring security clearance or were suspected of specific acts of espionage. "Both the CAUT and NFCUS have been advised that there is not now and will not be any general surveillance of university campuses."[19] On the surface it looked as though the situation had improved significantly.

By late autumn of 1963, however, it was apparent that, while the government and the RCMP intended to be more careful in the future, their basic outlook on the role of the Force in political matters had not changed. The general public had little opportunity of knowing in which direction events were moving because of the extreme secrecy in which RCMP operations were shrouded. On November 28, 1963, Douglas Fisher attempted, without success, to get a motion passed by the House of Commons instructing the Department of Justice to table correspondence that the RCMP had sent to a right-wing organization known as Alert Service.[20] The RCMP had previously acknowledged that they co-operated with Alert Service, which specialized in fighting the "communist menace," and Fisher produced some substantial circumstantial evidence that the Force had provided Alert Service with a list of alleged subversive organizations which Alert then published. Since it had been RCMP and government policy not to reveal to Parliament or the public which organizations were considered subversive, Fisher alleged that the RCMP provided information to Alert Service, a private right-wing group, which they denied to Parliament itself. Whether or not Fisher's allegation was correct neither Parliament nor the public ever discovered, because the government refused to disclose the relevant correspondence. The reasoning of some of the M.P.'s who contributed to the debate on the issue typified the attitude of all too many politicians about the degree of latitude which should be given to the RCMP. Gord Aiken, for instance, said:

> I do not think we can direct the RCMP as to how they operate. If they choose to operate in this manner, then I do not think we can prevent it. For example, if we asked the CIA either to acknowledge or deny that they had anything to do with flying of explosives into Cuba by the two Canadians who were recently arrested there, I do not think they would do so, and I certainly would not expect them to.[21]

Over the next three years the government and the RCMP were more careful than before and the former paid more lip service to the necessity of protecting people's civil rights. Complaints and controversies concerning RCMP activities were less frequent than in 1962 and 1963, which indicated that although spying on the campuses and within left-wing organizations was still going on, it was proceeding in a more circumspect and much less wholesale fashion. However, the situation remained far from satisfactory as far as the CAUT and other civil rights advocates were concerned. The government refused to divulge the new directions regarding security in the public service.[22] The CAUT received no formal complaints during this period concerning general RCMP surveillance on campuses but did hear unofficial accounts which caused them some concern. One was the report of a member of the secretarial staff of a university who revealed that she had been employed by the RCMP to make reports to them based on information she might receive in the course of her duties.[23] The CAUT and other groups were also concerned about the difficulties experienced by academics who could not accept university posts in Canada because they could not obtain security clearance to enter the country.

Continued complaints and official concern about both the effectiveness and possible shortcomings of Canada's security system prompted the government to appoint a Royal Commission on Security by an Order-in-Council of November 16, 1966. The commission was empowered "to make a full and confidential inquiry into the operation of Canadian security methods and procedures and, having regard to the necessity of maintaining (a) the security of Canada as a nation; and (b) the rights and responsibilities of individual persons, to advise what security methods and procedures are most effective."[24]

One of the three commissioners was M. J. Coldwell, former leader of the CCF, and his appointment was looked upon by many as a clever ploy to silence left-wing critics of the government's security policies. The appointment was completely safe from the government's point of view because, while Coldwell had been for most of his life a moderate leftist, by 1966 he was an old man unlikely to have any shocking progressive ideas. That Coldwell accepted the appointment and with it many of the conservative assumptions upon which the inquiry was based was proof of the fact that he no longer had any significant quarrels with the prevailing economic and political system.

The Report of the Royal Commission on Security was submitted to the Governor in Council in October 1968, and an abridged version for public consumption was published in June 1969. The report was a rationalization for the contentions of the government and the RCMP that the maintenance of an elaborate security system should be a high priority. A striking feature of the report was its assumption that the interests of Canada and those of the United States were virtually identical and that Canadian security measures should be planned with this in mind.

The United States is the leader of the western alliance in terms of military, economic and political power. As a member of this alliance with special relationships in many fields and an open frontier with the United States, Canada has a serious responsibility to ensure that its territory is not used as a base for the mounting and direction of foreign espionage and subversive operations against the United States, and that Canada is not a safe haven for foreign agents, or a route for infiltration into the United States. Quite apart from membership in the alliance, it is in the Canadian national interest to assist with the defence of North America against threats to internal security.[25]

The report made other assumptions which indicated that the commissioners, like the RCMP, were not only concerned with preventing actual acts of espionage or sabotage against the State but were also interested in frustrating the efforts of any groups who were dedicated to fundamentally changing the economic and political system. The Quebec separatist movement was considered a potential threat partly because some Communists and Trotskyists were interested in it.[26] Attempts by Communists to gain support were looked upon as subversive activities worthy of police attention.

The forms of communist subversive activity in Canada are varied, ranging from efforts to develop front organizations to attempts to *subvert individuals* in government, mass media, the universities, the trade unions, emigre and ethnic groups and political parties. Such activities are assisted by the fact that the communists are able to *exploit and exaggerate existing elements of social unrest and dissent concerned with a variety of appealing causes.* Some facets of their operations are worthy of special mention. First, activities in universities and trade unions appear at present to be of special significance. Half the population is under twenty-five and activities in the universities will have a considerable effect on the national climate of opinion in future years.[27] [Emphasis added.]

Presumably the implication was that radicals who demanded fundamental solutions to social problems should be curtailed by the security apparatus of the State and that the same apparatus would take a hand in moulding "the national climate of opinion in future years."

The attitude of the commissioners towards immigration followed the same line of reasoning. They noted that certain people might be undesirable as immigrants because "their past records of activities or associations may suggest that they are likely to behave in ways which may be detrimental to the security of Canada."[28] The report again emphasized the responsibilities of Canada to her allies. "In the area of immigration policy, because of the open border with the United

States, this responsibility is of special importance."[29]

The commissioners found the RCMP wanting in many respects in the field of security. Their criticisms centred on the belief that the RCMP were too inflexible and lacked the necessary sophistication to carry out effective security work. The report recommended a security service that would be civilian in nature and completely separate from the RCMP. The type of service recommended by the commissioners would undoubtedly have been more sophisticated than the RCMP, but the way they recommended it be controlled may also have made it more dangerous.

> We have considered arrangements that might be appropriate for the control of the Security Service. Although the Service must remain part of the executive arm of government and must be generally responsive to the orders of the government, arrangements must be made to provide the Head of the Service with some independence, especially in circumstances in which he may feel that orders (to provide information, for example) may be inappropriate. This independence must rest on some security of tenure, perhaps similar to that held by the Governor of the Bank of Canada, and upon clear and public terms of reference which include provision for the disclosure of information at his discretion.[30]

Lest people think this recommendation naive, the commissioners also recommended the creation of a Security Review Board to which the head of the Security Service would make annual or semi-annual reports. The board could then draw matters it considered appropriate to the attention of the prime minister, but it would not be accessible to complaints from the public. The report ruled out the possibility of a parliamentary committee performing this role,

> partly because, if the committee were to carry out its tasks in a meaningful way, its members would need formal security clearance. On general grounds we think it inappropriate to subject private Members of Parliament to these procedures, and in addition we foresee great complications if a Member nominated by a political party were ever deemed unacceptable on security grounds.[31]

The Report of the Royal Commission triggered considerable controversy throughout the country. It was attacked from the left for its conservative assumptions and its callousness towards civil liberties. Traditionalists also attacked many of the recommendations because they felt they down-graded the RCMP. The government moved cautiously towards adopting a modification of some of the report's recommendations without stepping too heavily on the toes of the RCMP.

Prime Minister Trudeau announced the government's intentions in the House of Commons on June 26, 1969.

> We are keenly aware that the RCMP are one of the most honoured and respected of Canadian institutions. The force has come to be recognized as one of the finest national police forces in the world, whose members, as the commissioners rightly state, are "carefully selected, highly motivated, and of great integrity."[32]

In describing the very minor changes the government intended to introduce, Trudeau noted that regular police duties and security duties were somewhat different in nature.

> It is therefore the government's intention, with the full understanding of the RCMP, to ensure that the Directorate of Security and Intelligence will grow and develop as a distinct and identifiable element within the basic structure of the force. . . The security service, under the Commissioner of the RCMP, will be increasingly separate in structure and civilian in nature.[33]

Trudeau went on to announce that the government would establish a Security Review Board with very limited power to review security cases involving employment, immigration and citizenship. He rejected the idea that such a board receive semi-annual reports from the head of the security service or that it have the right to draw pertinent matters to the attention of the prime minister. It was clear that the only significant thing likely to happen was that the RCMP security service might become somewhat more sophisticated and efficient in the future.

Since 1969 the RCMP have probably been more active in spying on and harassing dissenters that at any time since the darkest days of the Cold War. This is the result partly of increased dissent throughout the country since 1969 and partly of the fact that the Trudeau government has been more willing than its predecessors to violate civil liberties, as it proved beyond question in Quebec in October 1970.[34] As relevant documents become available, future historians may well decide that the Trudeau government of 1968-1972 had a worse record on civil liberties than any peacetime government since the R. B. Bennett regime of 1930-1935. Too often the RCMP and many other government departments and agencies have operated and continue to operate on the assumption that what is good for the United States is good for Canada. The RCMP and immigration officials have been most guilty of this in recent years. Now that it has become almost respectable to denounce the war crimes perpetrated by the American military in Vietnam, Canadians should be reminded that only a short time ago many of our politicians and much of the Canadian state apparatus looked upon refugees from the American military as undesirable immigrants and upon people who assisted them as subversive. Now that Canadians are congratulating themselves for having provided a haven for draft dodgers and deserters, they should also be reminded that if the politicians had followed the inclinations of RCMP and immigration officials many of these people would have died in Vietnam or languished in American prisons.

Federal authorities in Canada were divided on the advisability of granting landed immigrant status to draft dodgers and deserters from the United States armed services. The most intransigent opposition came from bureaucrats at all levels of the Department of Manpower and Immigration. These people have traditionally been among the worst political neanderthals in the employ of the Government of Canada. The petty bureaucrats at the lower levels of the department were especially notorious for harassment of people whom they considered to be out of favour with the United States Government. In many instances they had to be kept under constant pressure even to obey government regulations, and they often used any discretionary authority they possessed in the most callous and tyrannical manner imaginable.

Until July 1968, deserters were barred from entering Canada but draft dodgers were allowed to apply for landed immigrant status and were supposed to be judged on the same basis as anyone else. After July, 1968, immigration officials were instructed that they could exercise their own discretion as to whether or not deserters should be accepted as immigrants. In practice there remained a considerable amount of discrimination against both classes of refugees, but especially against deserters, for whom the difficulty of gaining acceptance varied from official to official and from month to month. What disturbed a great many Canadians were frequent charges that immigration officials and RCMP officers were co-operating with American military authorities and the FBI in preventing deserters from finding refuge in Canada. The actions of immigration officials became especially oppressive during late 1968 and early 1969 when a controversy was brewing over the issue which would eventually compel the immigration authorities to adopt a much more lenient attitude towards deserters.

In February 1969, five students from Glendon College at York University went to the United States. Then, posing as American deserters, they applied for landed immigrant status at five different border points. All five were rejected, and two were handed over to American authorities by Canadian immigration officials. If they had been real deserters, they would have faced stiff prison sentences. As these events became known, they sparked heated exchanges in Parliament and the press, and the resulting pressure from the public forced the government to adopt a more humane policy.

At first Allan MacEachen, minister of manpower and immigration defended the right of immigration officials to bar deserters from Canada and confirmed that it was common procedure to co-operate with American authorities in apprehending such people. In answer to a question from Arnold Peters in the House of Commons on February 17, 1969, MacEachen stated that he had read a report on the events involving the Glendon students and saw nothing amiss.

> I concluded that the officers had behaved properly and in accordance with the regulations. The action they took in advising their United States counterparts is one which I understand is routine at the border.[35]

In the next few weeks MacEachen got himself into hot water continuously. His remarks revealed that there were secret guidelines in the hands of immigration officials which, in effect, encouraged them to use their discretionary authority to bar deserters. MacEachen not only insisted that his departmental officials were legally justified in barring deserters but implied that they might be morally obligated to do so. In a heated exchange before the United Church's board of evangelism and social service on February 20, MacEachen asserted that there was a provision in the immigration regulations which could be applied to deserters: "This applies to someone from another country who is escaping his duty under the constitution of that country...It is something of great moral significance."[36] MacEachen went on to say that otherwise qualified immigrants could be disqualified if they had "substantial contractual obligations in their country of origin."[37] This provoked Toronto lawyer Vincent Kelly into retorting, "How can you say that a minor of 18 caught in the draft against his will has entered a contract?"[38]

MacEachen and the forces he represented had underestimated the extent of the opposition to the Vietnam war and to the government's subservience toward the United States. Many newspapers, most notably the Toronto *Star*, came out on the side of the war resisters. Several prominent Liberals denounced the government's policy. Leaders of the United Church and other religious organizations applied incessant pressure. In Toronto, citizens who could hardly be accused of having subversive tendencies formed the Committee for Fair Immigration Policies. Members included Charles Templeton, Robert Fulford, June Callwood and Rev. Gordon Stewart of the United Church's board of evangelism and social service. Similar committees were organized in Vancouver, Montreal, Ottawa and other cities. It was clear that the tide of opinion on the Vietnam war had irrevocably changed.

In the debate over the admission of deserters, a great many facts were made known to the general public which had previously been generally known only to the federal authorities, their victims, and left-wing political circles. A Toronto *Star* editorial of May 7, 1969, pointed out that not only were deserters being denied entry but that "draft resisters are running into unprecedented trouble confirming their status as landed immigrants."[39] On the same day the *Star* carried an article by Stephen Clarkson, Liberal candidate for mayor of Toronto in 1969. Clarkson was sharply critical of immigration and RCMP officials.

Equally disturbing are reports of harassment by RCMP officers of those waiting weeks for approval of their immigrant status.

And once the RCMP gets into the picture can the FBI be far behind? Cases have been documented of the RCMP turning over information on American "visitors" to U.S. authorities who then use this as evidence against the refugees should they return for a visit to the U.S.[40]

Clarkson went on to demand a clear-cut, liberal immigration policy and a clarification of the role of the RCMP in matters of immigration and of their relationship to the FBI.

This type of mounting public pressure finally compelled the government to capitulate on the issue. They conducted a major re-examination of immigration policy and announced later in the year that deserters were to be treated on the same basis as any other immigrants. The capitulation was a partial victory for the anti-war movement and for those Canadians most concerned about maintaining independence from the United States.

Despite this victorious public campaign of 1969, we cannot assume that RCMP and immigration officials changed drastically. There has been ample evidence since then to suggest the opposite, even though only a very few of the most notorious cases ever come to public attention. One incident occurred in British Columbia on January 25, 1970, when three deserters from the United States army who were legally resident in Canada were, in effect, kidnapped by RCMP officers and, with the knowledge and assistance of local immigration officials, turned over to American military police at the Huntingdon-Sumas border crossing. The RCMP picked up the three Americans in a highway restaurant and transported them to RCMP headquarters in Chilliwack. From there they took them to the Huntingdon (B.C.)-Sumas (Washington) border crossing where K. A. Smith, the senior immigration officer on duty, interrogated them. Later RCMP officers escorted them to the border. One of the deserters, John Keeger, managed to escape custody and make his way back to Canada. The other two, Charles Leonard and Earl Hockett, were imprisoned in a United States military stockade. The actions of both the RCMP and immigration officials were illegal and clear violations of government regulations, and when the incident became public such an outcry was raised that the federal government had to appoint Judge Ernest J. C. Stewart of B.C. County Court to be a one-man commission of inquiry.

The RCMP officers involved claimed they thought they were acting on behalf of the immigration authorities, and the immigration authorities insisted that the incident had been the responsibility of the RCMP.[41] K. A. Smith, the immigration officer who interrogated the three Americans, said that he felt the entire affair had been conducted by the RCMP and that it was not up to him to question their actions. "I felt it was their case and that they [the RCMP] may be interested in them from their point of view whatever that point of view may be."[42] He later stated, "I have no jurisdiction over the RCMP and I wouldn't question their judgement on a case."[43]

E. M. Russell, counsel for the department of manpower and immigration, went further than Smith and claimed that the deportation "had all been pre-arranged between the RCMP and American authorities."[44] Russell pointed out that Smith had not accompanied the three to the border but had handed them over to the RCMP outside the Canadian immigration building after determining that their entry into Canada had been legal. "If he was taking part in any deportation he would have accompanied the three Americans to the border."[45]

Russell also pointed out that the RCMP knew through radio conversations with American authorities that there was an FBI warrant out for the arrest of Keeger and that all three were deserters.

Other testimony indicated, however, that the immigration authorities were by no means blameless in the affair and that this case was just one of many in which people had been illegally returned to the United States. K. A. Smith revealed that he had told Kreeger's lawyer, Donald Rosenbloom, over the telephone that Kreeger was not in the immigration office at a time when he was there. Percy W. Booker, an official from the immigration office at Douglas, B.C., another border point, said it was a "well-known fact" that Americans were occasionally deported without going through the procedures required by law. (Legally no one can be deported without a special inquiry under the Immigration Act.) Booker said, "I can't name names, but I know it has happened on one or more occasions."[46]

It became clear from the testimony of John Kreeger and the RCMP officers involved that the RCMP had collaborated with American authorities in carrying out the illegal deportations. Kreeger testified that Peter Ediger, the radio operator for the Chilliwack detachment of the RCMP, informed him that he would be deported because of his absence from the United States Army for more than 30 days and that the FBI would be waiting at the border. (It turned out to be a United States naval shore patrol.) RCMP testimony varied from claims that the RCMP had merely been responding to a request from the immigration authorities to the ludicrous assertion that the three Americans had returned voluntarily to the United States. E. A. Dunkerley, the civilian radio operator for the RCMP in the Abbotsford-Sumas district, testified that K. A. Smith of the immigration department had called to request RCMP assistance in turning three Americans over to United States authorities.[47] Corporal William Kuzmuk of the Chilliwack detachment claimed that the three deserters returned to the United States willingly.[48] Constable Richard Stade, who helped escort Kreeger and his companions to the border, testified that he had forgotten the RCMP regulation that prohibited the deportation of American deserters.[49] He also claimed to be unaware that deportation papers must be served on people being deported from Canada.

The report of Judge E. J. C. Stewart, made public on June 25, 1970, found that the actions of the immigration officials and the RCMP had been illegal though not part of a conspiracy planned in advance. The judge described the actions of January 25 as "a mixture of coincidence, misunderstanding and confusion."[50] He laid much of the blame on K. A. Smith, the Canadian immigration official, but also directed considerable criticism at RCMP personnel. Stewart stated that Constable Dyck, who had originally arrested the three Americans, "should certainly have realized that no one is subject to arrest in Canada for desertion from the U.S. armed forces."[51] He also found that there "was liaison, if not active collaboration, between the RCMP and U.S. military authorities" but no concerted plot between the RCMP and the FBI.[52] He severely criticized E. A. Dunkerley, the RCMP civilian radio operator, whom he described as "A man who reports his own inferences and conclusions rather than the facts on which he bases them."[53] He called Dunkerley's evidence "colored," and said that Dunkerley had failed "to disclose all he knew."[54]

In spite of all the unfavourable publicity surrounding the illegal deportation of the three Americans, other incidents have occurred since 1970. One, involving a former member of the Black Panther Party, Edwin Hogan, happened on October 23, 1972.[55] Hogan, who had come to Canada after escaping from an Ohio prison, had been scheduled for deportation and had been going through the regular appeal procedures. Hogan lost his appeal before the Immigration Appeal Board, but he was legally entitled under the Immigration Appeal Board Act to file an additional appeal before the Federal Court of Canada within 15 days. Hogan was denied his legal rights by being spirited out of the country by immigration officials and RCMP personnel. Hogan's lawyer, Charles Roach, did not learn of the decision of the Immigration Appeal Board until after his client had been illegally deported.

In the area of general surveillance, the RCMP seem to have stepped up their activities since 1970 and the imposition of the War Measures Act. In an interview in May 1971, Solicitor-General Jean-Pierre Goyer stated that the government was reconsidering its 1963 policy instructions about general surveillance of campuses.

> The 1963 policy is no longer firm. It is open to public debate. We will have to make a decision.[56]

In the same interview Goyer referred to the Quebec crisis of October 1970, and implied that such crises justified increased RCMP activities on campuses. "Do you feel we should have reservations in Canada where people feel they can do as they wish, and act in a way that represents a threat to society . . . a security risk?"[57]

Prime Minister Trudeau had previously implied, on a United States television show in December 1970, that most violent political disturbances were begun by people connected with universities. "It's apparent that if the revolutions and the revolts are going to begin on campuses . . . if the instigators of violent dissent are going to find their natural milieu there, that there can be no more exception for the intellectual part of the community in the name of academic freedom than there can be for you and me in the name of our freedoms."[58]

A survey by the Canadian Press about the same time as Goyer's interview indicated that the government had probably already "loosened the leash" considerably on the RCMP as far as campus activities were concerned. Many university officials and student leaders contacted in the Canadian Press survey insisted that RCMP "fishing expeditions" were being carried on despite the directives of 1963. Dr. J. D. Eaton, dean of student affairs at Memorial University in Newfoundland, asserted that it would be "naive" to think that the RCMP were not "already on campus."[59] Similar convictions were expressed by several leaders of student associations.

Another embarrassing case for the RCMP involved the

family of W. A. Wilson, head of the Ottawa bureau of the *Montreal Star*. Wilson had been allowing newly arrived draft evaders and resisters from the United States to stay at his home. On the afternoon of March 4, 1970, Constable J. C. Benfield of the RCMP called at the Wilson home to enquire about the whereabouts of an American deserter. Neither Wilson nor his wife was at home, so Benfield proceeded to question their 17-year-old son and 13-year-old daughter. The questioning concerned not only the whereabouts of the deserter but also why the Wilsons helped deserters and how they got involved in providing assistance.[60] Annoyed that the police should be questioning children about the perfectly lawful activities of their parents, Wilson complained to Solicitor-General McIlraith and then took advantage of his prominence as a newspaperman to raise a well-publicized ruckus over the affair. McIlraith was forced to admit that the behavior of the police officer had been improper but claimed that this type of thing was not general.[61]

The RCMP spied on and harassed the National Farmers' Union (NFU) off and on during the years 1970-1972. Founded in 1969 as an amalgamation of farm unions in several provinces, the NFU is the most militant farmers' organization in Canada. Frequently during the 1970-1972 period, the NFU arranged mass demonstrations to publicize their grievances and put pressure on governments. In their surveillance of the NFU, the RCMP not only gathered information on members suspected of being "subversive" but also discredited the NFU in the eyes of many farmers. In these efforts, the RCMP security service co-operated with right-wing extremists who had connections with the Canadian Intelligence Service, a group who claim Prime Minister Trudeau is a Communist and who are notorious for the distribution of hate literature.

Most of the RCMP activity in connection with the NFU took place in Alberta, though there were also signs of such activity in other provinces. In Alberta, there was more controversy than elsewhere among the farming population about the merits and demerits of the NFU after it was founded in 1969. The Farmers' Union of Alberta (FUA), unlike farm unions in Saskatchewan, Manitoba and Ontario, did not become part of the NFU but instead amalgamated with the Alberta Federation of Agriculture to form Unifarm. The FUA took the majority of its members with it into Unifarm, which represented the conservative wing of the farm movement, but a minority of former FUA supporters joined the NFU and proceeded to organize locals in Alberta. From the beginning there was intense competition and considerable bitterness between Unifarm and the National Farmers' Union. The NFU has had a more difficult time establishing itself in Alberta than elsewhere because of the competition from Unifarm, which has always been favoured over the NFU by the provincial government, and because of the fact that Alberta farmers tend to be more conservative than their counterparts in other provinces.

After the NFU organized a particularly militant march on the Alberta Legislature in the spring of 1970, the RCMP stepped in and began questioning farmers about leading personalities in the NFU. There had already been an extremely hostile reaction to the march in the daily press, along with charges by Unifarm leaders that the NFU was communistic. The attorney-general of Alberta had also entered the fray by stating publicly that the Riot Act should have been read. Under the circumstances, questioning by the RCMP at this time undoubtedly helped to create the impression in the minds of many farmers that the NFU was under Communist influence. NFU President Roy Atkinson says RCMP plainsclothesmen soon began attending public meetings sponsored by the NFU.[62]

By this time the RCMP were already working with right wingers inside the NFU organization. In early 1970 three leading NFU activists—Bob Cheshire, a member of the national board from Alberta; James Rawe, Alberta director of organization; and Bert Simmons, NFU co-ordinator for British Columbia—got it into their heads that the NFU was strongly influenced by Communists and partially financed from Communist sources. The three were obviously obsessed with what they perceived to be the "Communist conspiracy." They began talking about the alleged Communist financing, and word of this got back to the top leaders of the NFU. Simmons admitted to NFU leaders in April 1970 that he had been spreading misleading rumours. James Rawe informed John Schmidt, agricultural columnist for the *Calgary Herald* and a noted right-winger, that he and Cheshire had contacted the RCMP security service and given them a report on the NFU.[63] Cheshire told Alberta members of the national board that he had been in contact with the RCMP security service.[64] Rawe claimed in his interview with Schmidt that he had made regular reports to the authorities for the last seven months he spent as Alberta director of organization.[65]

A vicious campaign of Red baiting against the leadership of the NFU led by Cheshire and Rawe throughout the remainder of 1970 seriously disrupted the NFU organization in Alberta. At the annual national convention in early December, Cheshire was again elected to the national board, but James Rawe was soon removed as director of organization in Alberta. Shortly after the 1970 convention, Cheshire and a supporter, Gloria Paquette, another Alberta member of the national board, resigned. They declared that the NFU was too radical, and Cheshire still alleged Communist influence.

Throughout 1971 Cheshire and Rawe conducted what amounted to a hate campaign against the NFU throughout Alberta. In March Rawe became a supporter of the Canadian League of Rights, an extreme right-wing group associated with the Canadian Intelligence Service,[66] whose research director, Pat Walsh, has long claimed to be a former S & I agent,[67] although the RCMP refuse to acknowledge it. Rawe and Cheshire distributed Canadian League of Rights and CIS hate literature throughout the areas of Alberta where NFU locals were located, to the point where NFU President Roy Atkinson felt called upon to decry Red baiting at the 1971 national convention. Such tactics gradually died down within the organization, but Cheshire and Rawe continued to spread their views throughout Alberta and much of the rest of the country. Cheshire made a national tour across Canada in the summer of 1972. They were not without assistance. It was discovered that some CIS literature was reproduced at the Agricultural Representative's Office in Bonnyville, Alberta.[68] The RCMP were also obliging. They were still interviewing Alberta farmers in the summer of 1972.[69]

Alberta was not the only province where the NFU came under RCMP surveillance. In the spring of 1970, they were questioning farmers in southwestern Saskatchewan about the activities of Don Kossick, an NFU organizer. RCMP plainclothesmen also attended NFU rallies in Saskatchewan. Fred Gudmundson, director of education and organization for the NFU, claims he has been followed by the RCMP on several occasions.

The role of the RCMP in Prince Edward Island, where Roy Atkinson was arrested during demonstrations in August 1971, is another interesting case. Premier Campbell of P.E.I. charged that the demonstrations were a conscious plot by outside agitators to upset the political situation and implied that his information came from the RCMP. The RCMP were also instrumental in advising Premier Campbell to concoct the notorious public order act which in effect gave the authorities the power to prohibit any public gathering of which they did not approve. The introduction of the act caused such a public uproar that it was eventually withdrawn.

During the years 1969-1972 the authorities were clearly worried about the growing support among farmers for the type of militant tactics engaged in by the NFU. It is apparent that the RCMP were used as one of the instruments in a scheme to discredit the NFU in the eyes of farmers. In carrying out this task the RCMP co-operated with right-wing extremists inside and outside the NFU. NFU President Roy Atkinson finally complained to the office of the commissioner of the RCMP and suggested that they confront NFU leaders openly if they thought they were subversives.[70] There was no response.

A final example of secret service activities by the RCMP is their abortive attempt to prepare a case against one David Orton for sedition in February 1971. Orton was then the main leader of the Regina local of a group that calls itself the Communist Party of Canada (Marxist-Leninist). The group claims to be Maoist though it is unlikely Mao would care to have anything to do with it. The incidents for which the RCMP wished to charge Orton for sedition occurred on November 22, 1969, about 15 months prior to the RCMP investigation. The events occurred at a seminar sponsored as a part of the Plain Talk series, which was part of a public affairs program sponsored by the University of Saskatchewan Regina Campus. The topic of this particular seminar was "Revolt *vs.* the Status Quo." Speakers taking part in panel discussions ranged from Orton to Chief Cookson of the Regina City Police to Maurice Shumiatcher, Q.C., a well-known right-wing lawyer in Saskatchewan. During the afternoon session, Orton was on a panel discussion with Shumiatcher and stated the CPC (ML) position that the only way to change the system was by armed revolution. At the evening session, which was addressed by Harry Magdoff, a visiting Marxist scholar from the United States, Orton denounced Magdoff as a liberal reformist and attempted to take over the microphone but was prevented from doing so by the chairman. The whole incident was of little consequence and no one seemed particularly concerned about it. Orton and his group were considered of no particular significance politically since they represented a handful of people at most.

It turned out, however, that the RCMP *were* concerned with Orton's behaviour on November 22, 1969, and that they had a long memory. On February 19, 1971, Sergeant McKenzie of the RCMP called on the university official who had been responsible for organizing the Plain Talk series and had chaired several of the sessions. McKenzie said he was conducting an investigation to prepare a case against Orton on a charge of sedition for remarks he made at the seminar on November 22, 1969. McKenzie quoted from extensive notes he had of Orton's remarks, which clearly indicated either that a police agent had been present at the seminar or that the RCMP were collaborating with someone who had been.

The proceedings had also been taped by the university, and McKenzie asked if the university would turn the tapes over to the RCMP. He also requested the co-operation of the university official who chaired the session at which Orton had attempted to take over the microphone as a witness against Orton should the case come to trial. The university official put McKenzie off by telling him he would have to consult his superiors before making any decisions. McKenzie left with the understanding that he would call back in a few days. After MacKenzie's departure, the university official informed his immediate superior of the visit from the RCMP and recommended that the university refuse to co-operate on the grounds that it would be a violation of academic freedom. His superior concurred in this view, and when McKenzie phoned a few days later he was informed that there would be no co-operation from the university. The matter was dropped.

The RCMP investigation of Orton proved for one thing that they were still spying on university campuses. Moreover, they had nothing on Orton in connection with any specific disturbances or conspiracies. Sedition is usually defined by reasonable people as inciting people to violent action under circumstances where such action is likely to occur. A good example would be making inflammatory remarks before an angry crowd during a strike or a political demonstration. Orton had not recommended any specific action but had merely stated he was in favour of bloody revolution before an academic audience the vast majority of which heartily disagreed with him. That such sentiments would be expressed by someone was hardly surprising given that the topic of the seminar was "Revolt vs. the Status Quo." That the RCMP did not begin the investigation until 15 months after the alleged offence is also significant, for by February 1971 the War Measures Act had been implemented for the first time in peacetime and the country was in a generally repressive mood.

The RCMP apparently decided that it was a good time to move against political dissenters and that David Orton should be locked up because he was a leading member of the CPC (ML). His remarks of November 22, 1969, were about the only things they could charge him with, and even then their case collapsed when the university authorities refused to co-operate.

In terms of openly proselytizing their political philosphy, the RCMP have been fairly silent in recent years. The government directive of 1963 ordering the Force to stop making political statements apparently still stands. However, some of the top officials have managed to get in a few licks on occasion, and a few ex-leaders of the Force have taken advantage of their retirement to make frequent public statements of a political nature. One of the more talkative has been William H. Kelly, who served for ten years, first as assistant director and then directory of the Security and Intelligence Directorate. Kelly retired in 1969 with the rank of Deputy Commissioner, Operations.

Testifying before the Commons Justice Committee on May 7, 1969, Deputy Commissioner Kelly blamed campus disturbances and unrest on outside agitators from other countries. He claimed that any serious demonstration at a university could usually be traced to the subversive influence of a militant leader. When asked by Douglas Hogarth, M.P., if the RCMP had specific evidence of subversive activity in campus disturbances of the past year, Kelly replied, "We have a feeling but no particular proof."[71] Kelly also lamented what he perceived to be developing contacts between students and organized labour and cited instances of students joining striking workers on picket lines. When Hogarth asked whether this was necessarily contrary to the national interest, Kelly replied, "If the leadership remains in the hands of people of the type now in control—yes."[72]

After his retirement in 1969, Kelly became well-known as a speechmaker and publicist. In an article entitled "Spying in Canada: A Special Report by an RCMP Expert," which was carried in the *Canadian Magazine* of November 29, 1969, Kelly emphasized the need to continue RCMP surveillance of university campuses lest students be recruited by the Soviet Intelligence Service and then in later life obtain influential positions in government or the business world. Kelly also claimed that the RCMP almost never made mistakes in investigating people for security clearance. "Out of literally millions of screening cases, only one real mistake has come to light."[73] This assertion was a blatant falsehood, of course, but what was frightening was his reference to "millions of screening cases." Unfortunately Kelly may not have been exaggerating. It has been estimated that 150,000 people were investigated for security reasons in 1963 alone.[74] An RCMP official once told a member of Parliament privately, "We have dossiers on so many people we have lost count of them."[75]

The *RCMP Quarterly* has remained almost completely silent about politics from 1963 to the present. However, the RCMP Veterans' Association has been under no inhibitions imposed by government policy, and their annual publication, *Scarlet and Gold*, has been very explicitly political. The politics espoused in *Scarlet and Gold* have been of the extreme right-wing variety. In the 1970 edition of *Scarlet and Gold*, editor W. E. G. Macdonald expressed his opinions of student groups and youthful dissenters in general:

> I feel that I express the private thoughts of most mature Canadians when I state my own. I am nauseated, disgusted, harassed and disappointed at the leaders of certain student groups in our society who have little of the dedication and loyalty which their forbears possessed. They are the yippies, hippies, activists, dissenters — many with long hair, dishevelled wearing apparel, and objectionable body odors.
>
> What do they want and why do they behave as they do? They have introduced propaganda words heretofore unknown, such as, "generation-gap" and "establishment", words that convey to the mature citizen little that has meaning in honesty or wisdom.[76]

Macdonald also expressed his disagreement with people who protested against the Vietnam war:

> The sights and sounds of the parades protesting the war in the Far East denouncing the activities of our powerful neighbor to the south, fill the streets. Yet the participants

must know in their hearts, if not in their minds, that this is of little concern to Canadians, whose past history has been one of friendly association with our protective cousins residing on the same continent.[77]

In an article entitled "A New Image for Policemen" in the 1971 edition of *Scarlet and Gold*, the editor lashed out at "permissiveness," which he alleged was a major threat to Canada, and also denounced organized labour:

Canada's cultural and economic development was halted for a period by her participation in two world wars. In the last decade we have encountered another setback engineered by a cult of permissiveness that spread from the homes of our citizens to the judicial administration of our laws.

There are hopeful signs that this latest, and to many people unnatural, obstacle to our advancement is entering its final stages. That it will leave in its wake broken bodies induced by drug participation and broken hearts by permissive or unwise parents is a price that we must reluctantly pay. The wave of illegal peace demonstrations, sex propaganda in printed or visual form, motion pictures that the use of so-called "nude" figures that for a time had a "surprise" appeal, are being shown in empty theatres, and it would seem that sanity and decency are now gaining public support.

Perhaps in the purely economic field our right to be called a strong viable nation is being interfered with by leaders in certain strongly entrenched groups who have cheapened and emasculated the word "labour". Because of strength in numbers, they have persisted with unreasonable demands to arrive at a goal where their demands more than double the gradual increase in the cost of living. That this is unfair to a wider population of unorganized citizens, and in particular to senior citizens, is evident. Since this is in the economic field and affects every person lving within our borders, it is a problem that will require determined action at the federal and provincial levels.[78]

The editor thereby revealed that the old distrust and even hatred for organized labour were not dead in RCMP circles. He also demonstrated that the generous assistance provided to *Scarlet and Gold* by Canadian Pacific, Seagrams and other large corporations was, from their point of view, money well spent.

Chapter 9
Maintaining the image: RCMP public relations

The RCMP have been one of the most successful police forces in the world in at least one respect: they have managed to become identified with the national interest to the point where criticism of the Force is considered by many people to be an unpatriotic act. Canada must be one of the few countries in the world where the main police force is considered a national symbol at home and is used to advertise the country abroad. The RCMP have a much more positive image, for instance, than the FBI in the United States, where J. Edgar Hoover may have been a folk hero to many but was a national embarrassment for millions of others. In Canada, the RCMP are looked upon as so much a part of the historical tradition of the country that tens of thousands of citizens sign a petition if the government attempts to alter the name of the Force. Even critics of the Force usually pay homage to it as an important part of our national heritage. In an editorial introducing Jack Ramsay's exposé of the Force in *Maclean's* magazine of July 1972, Peter C. Newman felt called upon to pay such homage: "In Canada's case, the Mountie symbolizes not merely law and order but Canada itself."[1]

How the RCMP have managed to project such a favourable image over such a long period of time must surely amount to the cleverest and most consistently successful public relations campaign in the history of Canada. Since the founding of the Force, RCMP leaders have placed a high priority on image-building and have usually been extremely resourceful by both negative and positive means to conserve and enhance a favourable image of the Force.

On the negative side, they have from the beginning shrouded their operations in such strict secrecy that few Canadians have any concept of what goes on inside the Force. This policy of secrecy was originally clamped on the Force to stop the unfavourable publicity resulting from complaints and criticisms of members, many of which appeared in letters to the public press. Such criticism led in 1875 to amendments to the

Mounted Police Act, which provided that members could be fined a month's pay or imprisoned for six months or both for, among other things, "communicating without the Commissioner's authority, either directly or indirectly to the public press, any matter or thing touching the force."[2] This type of regulation goes on piling up to the present day. Section 4 No. 1156 of the Commissioner's Standing Orders, 1970, lists 42 things which RCMP members are forbidden to do, including:

1156(33) write material for publication in any shape or form which relates to the Force, its work or history, or give information to anyone else who desires to do so, without first obtaining permission from the Commissioner; and all material permissibly written shall be submitted for the Commissioner's approval before publication.

1156(34) give information of any kind concerning the work or administration of the Force, or any department of the federal or provincial governments to the public, by radio, television, an address to a gathering, or by any other medium of communication, without the permission of the Commanding Officer or Office Commanding; the application for such permission to be accompanied by short summary of the remarks to be made.

1156(35) discuss in an unauthorized manner with anyone any matters dealing with the work or duties of the Force or the services of any member, or any other matter which may come to his notice by virtue of his being a member of the Force.

1156(36) give a character or other reference in any form to any member about to be discharged from the Force, or to any ex-Member, or anyone else who is or has been employed by the Force, except as provided in the Standing Orders of the Commissioner.

1156(37) supply any information to the public, either in writing or otherwise, concerning the character, ability, or service in the Force of any member or ex-member, or of anyone else other than a public servant who is or has been employed by the Force.

Obviously little or nothing can get out to the public which is not approved at least by a Commanding Officer and usually the Commissioner himself.

This obsession with secrecy is not confined to the internal operations of the contemporary Force. The history of the

Force is also guarded with the utmost secrecy. Researchers are allowed into the papers of most government departments and agencies, including the armed forces, by virtue of the so-called "thirty year rule," whereby all papers at least thirty years old are open for inspection without restrictions and more contemporary material can often be examined with special permission. The only exceptions are papers on defence research involving atomic energy, germ warfare and weapons systems, and RCMP files. *All* RCMP files, no matter how old, dealing with strikes, labour unrest, espionage, subversion and general security and intelligence work were, until October 1971, closed to researchers except by special permission of the RCMP. This permission was granted only to friends of the Force who had been very carefully screened and even then under very strict stipulations. The stipulations provided that any material used must be examined by the Commissioner or his appointee, who would pass judgement not only on whether the material could be used but also on the exact context in which it was used. In 1971 the RCMP, apparently embarrassed by their situation, removed sensitive material from the Public Archives of Canada and then opened what remained to researchers. Since no serious scholar or journalist of integrity would work under the stipulations, in effect until 1971, the result was that only sycophantic friends of the RCMP were allowed access to inside information on many of the most important aspects of RCMP history. Critics of the Force and objective scholars have had to dig up their information elsewhere; nevertheless they have sometimes been amazingly successful at revealing at least the tip of the iceberg. When Stanley Hanson, for instance, wrote a thesis on the Estevan strike and riot of 1931, he had to observe that "the records of the RCMP would have been of inestimable assistance. However, because they are held by the Special Investigation Branch of the force, these records are inaccessible for research purposes."[3] Fortunately, Hanson was able to reconstruct some of the more blatant acts of the RCMP despite their attempts to keep their history hidden. However, for the most part the RCMP have written their own history more than any other institution, private or public, in our society.

Nearly all the literature dealing with the RCMP in Canada reflects the extent to which the Force has written or directed the writing of its own history. About half the books on the subject are histories or memoirs by retired top-ranking officers of the Force. The other half are by people who worked in close collaboration with the RCMP hierarchy, and most of them romanticize and glorify the Force to the point of absurdity. The prefaces and acknowledgements in these books range from obsequious to hilarious. Thus R. C. Fetherstonhaugh, who wrote *The Royal Canadian Mounted Police* in 1938, allegedly based on the records and documents of the Force, pays tribute to the late Commissioner, Major-General Sir James H. MacBrien, "who kindly read the script and thus made sure that in the descriptions of events throughout the years the point of view of the Police was correctly presented."[4] Nora Kelly, in *Men of the Mounted* in 1949, acknowledged the assistance of Commissioner S. T. Wood, "who kindly had the manuscript read and so made sure that the information contained therein was correctly presented from the point of view of the Mounted Police."[5] In 1954 Alan Phillips dedicated *The Living Legend* "to those officers and men of the Royal Canadian Mounted Police who helped so much with the researching of this book."[6]

An examination of these books indicates how heavily the authors must have depended upon RCMP versions of history. Frequently their descriptions of controversial events involving the RCMP bear little relation to the facts. For instance, they describe the Winnipeg General Strike as an OBU revolutionary conspiracy years after a Royal Commission and numerous other sources have proven otherwise. They regularly blame instances of violence on strikers and portray the RCMP as the saviours of decency and justice. Phillips describes the Estevan riot of 1931 as having been consciously provoked by the Communists and finds the RCMP blameless for any loss of life involved. In all their descriptions of RCMP involvement in labour disputes, the authors portray the Force as neutral upholders of law and order and ignore or deny the fact that they consistently sided with the employers. Phillips' account of the Regina riot of July 1, 1935, takes the cake on this score. He accepts without question Commissioner MacBrien's claim that the On-to-Ottawa Trek had been planned as the prelude to a revolution and asserts that the riot had been planned days in advance by the Trek leaders:

> Undercover reports to the RCMP told of piles of stones being cached in alleys. Elevator operators were taking bricks to the roofs of buildings bordering the square. The camp

workers were arming themselves with clubs, knives and flails, and a few guns.[7]

Phillips then insists that the riot began on Market Square when the police were ambushed while trying to arrest the Trek leaders. "Immediately, from the roofs and windows above, from all sides, iron, cement, bricks and stones rained upon the police"[8] Phillips' entire description, vivid as some may find it, bears little resemblance to what actually happened in Regina on July 1, 1935.

The saddest thing about these books is how typical they are of literature about the RCMP. The type of propaganda found in them is accepted at face value and pushed not only by the RCMP themselves but by the mass media. The glorification of the RCMP has always been a favourite subject of the media in Canada because of the romantic conceptions surrounding the early history of the Force. Children's literature, including school textbooks, has hammered away at the theme for over half a century. Generations of Canadians have been raised to believe sincerely that the Force is and has always been an incorruptible institution which never fails to live up to its motto: Maintenant le Droit.

The force has not left responsiblity for its image solely to retired officers and sycophantic authors. It has always devoted considerable resources to vast public relations campaigns by its own members. Probably the most popular of these among the public has been the famed Musical Ride, which became perhaps the most entertaining and most susccessful public relations stunt ever devised by any police force in the world. First devised by cavalry regiments, the musical ride was adopted and perfected by the RCMP. Requiring extremely well-trained horses and superb horsemanship, the Musical Ride became a popular public attraction at fairs and exhibitions throughout Canada. The Ride also made extensive tours of the United States and Britain. It was discontinued in 1939 because of the exigencies of the war but was reinstated in 1948 by considerable popular demand.

The Force has also exploited to the full its identification with royalty and has cultivated it with great success from the early years of the NWMP. The word "Royal" came to be part of the name of the Force because of its service to the Empire during the Boer War. Contingents from the Force have attended every coronation, jubilee and similar celebration held in

Great Britain ever since, and always accompany the Sovereign and other royal personages on tours of Canada. This identification of forces in the Empire with British royalty was strongly encouraged by Britain, of course. And when RCMP troops were a big hit at ceremonial occasions in Britain, which they usually were, the news was widely reported in Canada. Fetherstonhaugh's history of the Force proudly boasts of the tremendous reception accorded the Mounties at the Coronation of King George VI and Queen Elizabeth:

> With the exception of the ovations to the King, the Queen and the members of the Royal Family, no roar of cheers exceeded that which greeted Assistant Commissioner S. T. Wood and the detachment of the Royal Canadian Mounted Police. There had been many proud moments in the Force's history, but none prouder than the occasion of that march through London, when the Empire voiced thunderous acclaim.[9]

On ceremonial occasions of this nature, the Sovereign sometimes authorized the issue of long service medals and other decorations for members of the RCMP and honoured the top-ranking officers by making them Members of the Order of the British Empire, Knight Commanders of the Most Honorable Order of the Bath and other orders denoting pomp and circumstance. Perhaps this identification with royalty helped as much as anything to establish the RCMP in the minds of Canadians as an almost sacrosanct institution, the epitome of the State itself. Even as this book is being written, the officers of the Force are preparing for another orgy of adulation when the Queen visits Canada in 1973 to celebrate the RCMP centennial.

The RCMP have always been exceptionally adept at injecting themselves into situations where they will be seen as symbolizing the essence of what Canada is supposed to mean. For instance, RCMP officers dressed in Review Order accompany judges when immigrants are sworn in as citizens. These ceremonies are usually reported in the local press and are sometimes covered in the *RCMP Quarterly* as well. Constable J. F. Bette described such a ceremony at Prince George, B. C., in the *RCMP Quarterly* of October 1951.[10] On this occasion Judge E. D. Woodburn treated the new citizens to a lecture "drawing attention to our beautiful democratic country" and pointing out that to keep Canada great "is why we use such care in seeing that only the right people become our citizens." Some of the judge's comments indicated that he was indulging fully in poetic license: "A land of good educational facilities, police forces for the public protection, perhaps the world's finest legal system, incorruptible officials, a land where the sick, the aged and the helpless are not forgotten and a land where racial and religious intolerance are little known." Constable Bette was greatly impressed and presumably the editors of the *RCMP Quarterly* were too: "We believe worthwhile work is being done here, and it is a pleasure for our Force to co-operate with what Judge Woodburn is trying to accomplish." The Constable might have noted at least one of the many ironies of the ceremony that took place in British Columbia in 1951: two of the new citizens were Japanese.

Members of the RCMP hierarchy worried about their image in the period immediately after World War II. They feared that many people, especially young people, did not respect the Force or "law and order" in general as much as they would like. They were probably correct in their assessment of the situation, but it is unlikely that they were aware of all the reasons for it. The Mounties had run roughshod over trade unionists and the unemployed for two decades between the wars and then had been the instruments of authoritarian and often arbitrary and unjust government policies during World War II. A great many young people must have been told by their parents or discovered for themselves that the RCMP did not exactly fit the textbook image they had got in school. A general wave of rebellion and dissatisfaction swept through Canada after the war, unrelated to the Force. At any rate, RCMP leaders were clearly worried and began devising schemes to boost public respect for the police in general and the Mounties in particular.

The most important scheme they devised, originally referred to as the "youth and police" program and eventually dubbed "Operation Citizenship," was positively Machiavellian in its cunning, for you could not really criticize it without appearing to be against motherhood itself and all the other "wholesome instincts." What grew to be "Operation Citizenship" began as a program of RCMP involvement in general youth activities and then quickly spread until it embraced almost the entire school system in some provinces. It began as a few scattered, well-meaning efforts by local RCMP personnel on the prairies, and was then seized upon by Commissioner S. T. Wood in his best cynical fashion and made a central part of the public relations efforts of the Force.

Sergeant W. H. Kelly outlined the "youth and police" program in the *RCMP Quarterly* of July 1946: "Commissioner S. T. Wood, C.M.G., felt that the Force, by a positive and sympathetic approach could lead our boys and girls to realize the true office of the policeman not as a person to be feared but as a friend and protector."[11] Kelly than proceeded to describe a well-organized and ambitious program co-ordinated by a few key men whose subordinates had the latest in audio-visual aids in order to make the best use of public relations techniques. Kelly boasted that the program had already reached over 100,000 children and pointed out how an RCMP officer had a great advantage over a civilian in addressing youthful audiences. "His uniform and the organization to which he belongs appeal strongly to young minds." The Mountie could depict exciting episodes in the history of the Force to illustrate his points and sometimes do even better than that: "To stimulate interest, police dogs also are shown to admiring youthful audiences, and in explaining a police dog's work, emphasis is placed on the animal's virtues as a searcher for lost children rather than its ability to locate illicit liquor or to track down fugitives." Kelly placed considerable emphasis on getting an audience into the right frame of mind, and cited an example of how one good con artist had introduced his subject by asking the assembled boys what, in their opinion, was the reason for the talks.

> The answers came thick and fast. To keep us off the streets. To keep us some place where our parents know we won't get into trouble. To see that we won't become juvenile delinquents. In a way all replies were correct, but the speaker, desiring to get away from that line of thinking in so far as program was concerned, stated that none was the answer he wanted.

The answer, believe it or not, was to tell the boys about the greatness of Canada. "He pointed out that members of the RCMP were quite competent to speak in this regard because they travel extensively in Canada and know the country well."

The "greatness of Canada" was undoubtedly a central theme of the ideology of the program, which was designed to portray Canada as the best of all possible worlds and the RCMP as grown-up Boy Scouts who were an indispensable part of it. "The topics discussed are calculated not only to instil in our boys and girls a wholesome attitude toward the police but to establish in their minds a realization that the laws and traditions of Canada are something of which to be proud; something to be maintained." Democracy was right in there too: "Developing the democratic ideal is the purpose of the RCMP program, and like all good seed it should eventually bear good fruit." It was not explained how a totalitarian organization could help people to develop the "democratic ideal."

Kelly claimed that the program, although not yet a year old at the time of his report in the *RCMP Quarterly,* was a whopping success. It was earning lavish praise in the press and from members of the public and the Force. He quoted the director of a boys' club as declaring, "You can believe me that the boys have developed a keener sense of admiration and respect for forces of law and order." According to Kelly, the program was probably even improving discipline in the schools. "It was found that on occasion a lecturer could assist, indirectly of course, in checking the antics of chronic troublemakers in the classroom." One officer reported that even the children of "foreigners" were changing their attitude. "An N.C.O. of 'D' Division, Manitoba, reports that the children there, many of whom are of foreign extraction, are showing a marked change in their attitude toward the police."

For years afterwards, the *RCMP Quarterly* carried editorial comments from the daily press praising the "youth and police" program to the skies. A typical one, from the *Ottawa Journal,* said: "Children need to be taught respect for law and order and to hear the story from a Mountie will likely impress them more than if the same story and ideas were told by their teachers."[12]

An article in the *RCMP Quarterly* of January 1950, entitled "Operation Citizenship," claimed that by then the program had involved 800,000 young people and was still going great guns. The article noted that some police officers had taken to studying public speaking and child psychology, and quoted the praise of Judge E. J. Heaney of the Winnipeg Juvenile Court: ". . . given the choice, a boy will make a hero of a policeman. And in return a policeman can teach youth a good deal, even if the activities are purely athletic."

While the RCMP are by no means averse to mounting public relations campaigns of their own, they have seldom been in a position where they had to rely solely on their own efforts. The close links they developed with the corporate interests in the nineteenth century have lasted to this day. That the large corporations have always taken a friendly interest in the Force is not surprising, considering the long and loyal service of the RCMP on behalf of Capital in its struggles with Labour. A glance through a few issues of *Scarlet and Gold*, the annual publication of the RCMP Veterans' Association, confirms the high regard which the corporate elite and the RCMP hierarchy hold for each other. It also affirms their ideological affinity. The 1969 *Scarlet and Gold* carried an article describing a police show put on by Eaton's Vancouver store to mark their centennial. The theme of the show was the policeman as a knight on a white horse protecting society from the forces of evil and sometimes from itself. Attorney-General Leslie Peterson was quoted as having high praise for the show and emphasizing "the need of greater awareness by the public of the need to support and assist law-enforcement agencies in a society where permissiveness and tendencies to rebel against authority are dominant."[13]

The 1969 issue of *Scarlet and Gold* also contained an article by N. R. Crump, Chairman of Canadian Pacific, and one by Joseph Shell for the House of Seagram with an introduction by Samuel Bronfman, Seagram's president. There were also articles contributed by the Bank of Nova Scotia and Molson's of Canada, and it was obvious that these large corporations had borne most of the cost of publishing *Scarlet and Gold*. An editor's note on the greatness of N. R. Crump mentioned that he was an honorary member of the Canadian Association of Chiefs of Police, that he was on the advisory board of the RCMP Veterans' Association, that "his interest in the history and welfare of the Force is deep and continuing" and that he often "detects interesting parallels between the origin and development of his great company and the original North West Mounted Police."[14]

Scarlet and Gold for 1968 had also contained pieces by Crump and Bronfman. Bronfman's article was entitled "Neighbours in Democracy — Canada and the United States," and was preceded by an editor's introduction which lavished praise on Bronfman and his empire.

The vast industrial organization which is headed by Samuel

Bronfman has demonstrated on many occasions its pride and confidence in the strength and influence for good of these neighbours working in harmony. His splendid organization, with large interests in both countries, has supported the best interests of both and, by its private benevolence and public interest in all worthwhile community efforts, gives ample evidence of the the just fruits of our democratic system.[15]

The editor explained that *Scarlet and Gold* was carrying the article because the publishers wished to "foster and promote respect and confidence in our proven system of government" and point with pride to the role of the RCMP "in maintaining the integrity of our institutions and establishing the rule of law and justice throughout our nation." What the editor neglected to mention was that the Bronfmans had got their start as bootleggers and smugglers in southeastern Saskatchewan during the Prohibition era. They had corrupted the provincial and local police forces and so controlled an entire region of the province that they were never successfully prosecuted, though the Crown did try on at least one occasion. Bronfman's article on this occasion sang the praises and lauded the stability of North American society.

In many European democracies, parties hostile to the established constitutional order have never ceased to enjoy a large measure of popular support. In North America, by happy contrast, there are practically no strong disaffected minorities.[16]

It is almost inconceivable that anyone could have written that in 1968, for although the minorities may not have been strong, they were large in number and they certainly were disaffected!

RCMP Headquarters leaves nothing to chance in dealing with the press. The Commissioner's Standing Orders include specific and detailed instructions on how to deal with the press. They also instruct local detachments to forward to headquarters any of the following types of items which might appear in the press:

- criticism of the Force and its personnel
- commendatory notices of the Force and its personnel
- criticisms and commendatory notices of the administration of the Force
- all editorial references to the Force, and the responsibilities

of the Force including those in which the Force is not mentioned by name
- press references to cases prosecuted or investigated by the Force
- editorial references to other police forces.

If a particular newspaper or news reporter tends to portray the Force in an unfavourable light, appropriate steps are taken to lean on the right people in an attempt to rectify the situation. While this may have little effect on principled editors, all too many newspapers in this country are in the hands of businessmen who are not in the least interested in honest journalism. Curiously, it is the better newspapers and magazines in Canada which have occasionally offered pointed criticisms of the Force.

Despite all efforts by the RCMP and their friends to prop up the image of the Force, it underwent a marked decline, as did that of other police forces, during the 1960s. Once people, particularly young people, began to question critically many aspects of our society they did not exempt the police. The rise of protest movements and a more militant attitude among students, Quebecois, workers and farmers led to clashes with the police and caused more and more people to realize whose interests the police in general and the RCMP in particular actually served. Minority groups like Indians and Metis, who had always been oppressed by the RCMP, began saying so and demanding changes in no uncertain terms as they became better organized. The RCMP seldom if ever admitted that any of the criticism was justified. More commonly they bemoaned the alleged evils of a permissive society and suggested that persons or groups who criticized the police were doing so for ulterior motives or at least from ignorance. Most public discussions of the problem by RCMP officials and publications stressed the notion that public relations had to be improved.

In addressing the 1960 conference of the Canadian Association of Chiefs of Police, Commissioner C. W. Harvison of the RCMP was critical of the press for supposedly co-operating with people who unjustly criticized the police. He also harped on one of the favourite themes of police officials, that repeated criticism destroys the efficiency of the police and, by implication, plays into the hands of the criminal elements. Harvison admitted that some criticism might be justified and could be eliminated by removing the grounds for complaint, but then went on to deal with the rest. "But un-justified criticism, repeated over and over again — as has been the case in recent years — if allowed to remain unanswered has, in my opinion, a strong adverse influence on the morale of our men."[17] The solution, then, was not to remove the grounds of complaint in most cases, because supposedly there were no such grounds, but rather to improve public relations techniques and strengthen the police as a pressure group.

I believe firmly that we need a stronger, better and more insistent voice than we have today — a voice that would speak seriously and thoughtfully on behalf of all those who are responsible for the administration of police forces — and indeed, for all policemen. An association, permanently and adequately staffed, could attempt to do for us what the Bar and Medical Associations do for those professions. Our views could, and should, be placed before legislators, the Bench, the Bar, the press and the public in a better, more helpful and more uniform manner than is now possible.

The conference agreed with Harvison and established a committee to implement his recommendations.

Despite all such efforts, public confidence in the police continued to dwindle throughout the 1960s and by the end of the decade RCMP officials were more concerned than ever about their declining image. RCMP Superintendent E. A. F. Holm, speaking before a police banquet in Victoria on October 19, 1968, blamed the declining image on the movie industry and the mass media. He singled out the CBC for special criticism and accused the network of portraying policemen "as being uncouth in both manner and appearance" in the TV series *Quentin Durgens, M.P.* Holm declared that the FBI or the Los Angeles Police Department would not allow such a thing to happen in the United States. He suggested that the Canadian Association of Chiefs of Police (C.A.C.P.) should step up their public relations efforts and also see to it that the CBC toed the line.

The C.A.C.P. should also take steps to arrange that any scripts depicting the police and their work are accurate and not the result of what some misguided script writer believes a policeman to be. Let's put an experienced policeman or two on the CBC staff for this purpose, the dividends would be most worthwhile.[18]

Holm also suggested an annual Police Week or Police Day across the country and asked his listeners to consider a suggestion by Sergeant Springate of the Montreal Police Department to the effect that the army, rather than the police, be used for "putting down large-scale mob action which borders in some instances on insurrection."

Superintendent Holm did not point at any particular group, aside from the mass media, as being responsible for the decline of confidence in the police. In an editorial accompanying Holm's speech, which was carried in *Scarlet and Gold* for 1968, however, the editor blamed the declining support for the police on elements in the media who catered to agitators of the Left.

> The monotonous garbage dispensed by certain openline radio broadcasters, as well as the news slanting liberties taken by the visual media, contains all too often the implication of support for the criminal, the student activist and phony peace-marching critic of Canadian and American foreign policies. The substance of many public utterances reveals a permissiveness given to left-wing agitators to voice their opposition to our democratic way of life, always with overtones of disrespect for the rule of law. Is it to be wondered that respect for the rules of law and good order are in danger? Public confidence in the dispersing of our laws and admiration of law-enforcement agencies is threatened by confusion rather than by a lack of support.[19]

Speeches by RCMP officials and items in their official publications reveal that they have not changed their thinking since 1968. Their response to criticisms is to deny that there are any grounds for them, to suggest that the criticisms are made for ulterior motives, or to suggest that the police could be projecting their "true image" more skillfully. The number of criticisms has increased. The critic to reach the widest audience in recent years was of course Jack Ramsay in his *Maclean's* expose of July 1972. The official RCMP response to Ramsay has been to deny that his criticisms have validity and at the same time to appear to be instituting extremely minor reforms which are almost totally without substance. The response to criticisms by Indian, Metis and other groups has been similar. It seems the only significant thing the RCMP have any intentions of changing is their advertising budget.

The centennial year has come none too soon for the hierarchy of the RCMP and their hard-line "law and order" supporters, who hope that the mounting criticism of recent years will be drowned out by the millions of dollars' worth of free publicity the Force will receive in the mass media. Governments will spend millions more glorifying the Force and have even arranged a Royal tour for the purpose. Saskatchewan alone, where the centennial celebrations are being turned into a tourist gimmick, will spend in excess of $100,000 to persuade anyone who can be persuaded that the RCMP is and always has been the greatest police force in the world. The RCMP themselves have a budget of $1 million for advertising and promotion during 1973. Government officials are also taking advantage of the centennial to provide school-children with an extra dose of misinformation about the role of the RCMP and the need for law and order. Saskatchewan Education Minister Gordon MacMurchy has directed that RCMP centennial calendars be placed in all schools and announced that schools will be encouraged to undertake special projects and activities to celebrate the centennial. MacMurchy's statement on the subject could not have been phrased better by the RCMP themselves:

> The history of the RCMP is an integral part of the history of Saskatchewan and the Centennial Year will provide a special motivation for the study of the province's early history. It will also provide a unique opportunity for the development of student attitudes of respect for law and order in our society.[20]

Similar campaigns are under way throughout most of Canada. The national media have already been inundated with propaganda. A sign of things to come was the *Canadian Magazine* of January 27, 1973, which was devoted almost entirely to glorifying the RCMP. The whole sickening barrage of propaganda is introduced by an article entitled "Mounties Are Fun" by Hartley Steward. Steward admits that the RCMP have been so secretive few people know much about them, but insists we have all missed out on a tremendous treat by being kept in the dark. "We found that the better you get to know the Mounties, the better you like them. When you've finished reading this issue, we hope you like them better, too."[21] Perhaps Steward should distribute copies of the magazine to the Indian and Metis communities of northern Saskatchewan or at trade union conventions. From what these groups know about the Mounties, they are anything but fun.

Chapter 10
Behind the image

Behind the red-coats, the Musical Ride and the romantic image of maintaining the right lies the real RCMP — the ordinary Mountie who carries out his day-to-day services to the people. To the Indian on a reserve in northern Saskatchewan who's been brutalized while in police custody or the counterculture youth who's been picked up in a car and punched out, then released without charge, the real image is not very nice. The phrase "police brutality," which came into vogue during the 1960s and 1970s, is not merely a trite expression used by flippant middle-class kids who like to imagine themselves persecuted. Harassment of youth in general, hippies in particular, and immigrants, especially U.S. draft-dodgers, has been very much a part of the recent RCMP image.

Aside from the comparatively petty acts of harassment which occur from time to time, the use of young people as paid informers is a particularly obnoxious feature of RCMP practice. On August 15, 1971, then Solicitor-General Jean Pierre Goyer insisted that the RCMP "wouldn't have a young person as informer on its payroll."[1] The case of a Cornwall youth who was "hired" as an informer is therefore an interesting one to examine, both in terms of the way the RCMP operated and in terms of the statements made by officials at the time the incident became public. On September 8, 1971, less than a month after Goyer made his statement, Robert Wayne Eadie, aged 21, revealed on a CBC television program that he had been a paid informer of the RCMP when he was 18. In telling of how he first became an informer, he said:

> One night I got picked up by the city police regarding intoxication and they called in the RCMP because they were aware that I knew people in the drug scene, and forced me by threatening that they would send me back to prison if I did not give them information regarding drugs. I had a choice to either come across with information or get busted by them, even as far as getting planted — drugs on me.[2]

Eadie stopped informing after he was beaten up by six men in Cornwall and, according to his story, denied police protection. In an interview with a *Globe and Mail* reporter on August 21, 1971, Eadies's father said that it was only after this beating that he and his wife became aware that their son was a police informer.

On September 9, RCMP Deputy Commissioner Geoffrey Mortimer confirmed that Robert Eadie had been an RCMP informer in Cornwall at the age of 18. His only comment on Eadie's charge of intimidation was "it is not a system the force uses but we have to investigate this claim he has made against an individual."[3] Solicitor-General Goyer ordered Commissioner W. L. Higgitt to investigate the allegations. When asked by reporters outside the House of Commons if the charges against the RCMP were to be investigated *only* by the RCMP, Mr. Goyer replied:

> At this stage yes. If I am satisfied by the report I will report to the House. If I am not satisfied I will look at other measures.[4]

He was satisfied with the report when it was made. A motion introduced by Frank Howard (NDP, Skeena) in the House calling for an inquiry by the Justice Committee was defeated when government supporters denied the necessary unanimous consent.

On September 17, Mr. Goyer made a reply to the charges based on the RCMP report. He said that, at the time Eadie became an informer he was 18 years and eight months old (not a juvenile under Ontario law); that no record existed of Mr. Eadie being arrested by the Cornwall police at the time (Is it likely, if the police had made such a deal with Eadie, that they would have recorded his arrest?); that between April 30, 1969, and February 18, 1971, Eadie helped the RCMP in forty successful drug cases and was paid $710 during that period; that his father had consented to the activity; and that he was never threatened or coerced.[5]

Although Mr. Goyer was happy with the investigation, the results of which got him off the hook politically, he told the Commons of a new policy regarding what he termed the "repugnant" practice of paying juvenile informers. The new standing instructions relating to juvenile informers which had been implemented by the RCMP on August 24 directed the RCMP to accept information on the initial contact, but to seek parental consent for any further information. "A juvenile shall not be assigned an informant's number, or paid money under any circumstances. Juveniles shall not be used to purchase drugs."[6] At the time the policy was implemented, there were six juvenile informers on the RCMP payroll.[7] Mr. Goyer defended the continuing use of informers, but said he did not know how many juvenile informers were supplying information without pay.

The interim report of the LeDain Commission on the nonmedical use of drugs made public in June, 1970, criticized the method of entrapment used by the RCMP in drug investigations. In this method, underground RCMP narcotics officers pose as young drug users to coax suspects into providing evidence. Despite the Commission's criticism, it would appear that this illegal method of obtaining evidence is still being used.

For police to investigate incidents involving police is a questionable procedure at best, and in actual practice it often serves only as a method of exonerating the police. In a tightly-knit military organization such as the RCMP, where the image is placed "above truth, justice and service to the people of Canada" (to use Jack Ramsay's words), what else can one expect? Surely it would make sense to have an independent committee carrying out such investigations if impartial justice was the desired result. The need is all the more glaring when we realize the lack of awareness on the part of the civil authority — the solicitor-general in the Eadie case — of what is actually going on within the Force.

In addition to the built-in safeguards afforded by the degree of secrecy under which the RCMP are permitted to operate, individual officers exercise a great deal of power over people simply through the way in which they choose to enforce the law. In many instances the officer is a law unto himself. Even the lowest-ranking member exercises a great deal of discretion in how he carries out his job. In addition the role and power of the police extend into the courts of law where the police act directly as prosecutors or indirectly as assistants to prosecutors. Either way, they have a great deal of influence over whether or not a person is convicted. Far from being impartial experts presenting evidence in an objective manner, they often have a vested interest in the outcome of a trial, as chapters 11 and 12 will show.

The use of this extensive and often arbitrary power is most pronounced in dealing with racial and other minorities. As Jack Ramsay says, "The easiest pinch for statistics is the Indian."[8] Racism, a vicious cancer afflicting large numbers of Canadians, is doubly odious in policemen because of the power they have over people. A quick look at jail statistics proves Ramsay's point about Indians and statistics.

Forty percent of men in Western Canadian jails or prisons are Indians, although Indians make up a much smaller fraction of Canada's population. In Northern Alberta, Indians number 20 percent of the population, but 40 percent of the jail and prison population.[9]

In Saskatchewan the situation is even worse. Indians make up 10 percent of the population but 50 percent of the jail and prison population.[10] The figures for women prisoners in Saskatchewan are even more disproportionate. Charges such as drunkenness or creating a disturbance, where there is leeway for discretion on the part of the officer as to whether or not he makes an arrest, are common among Indians and Metis. Since more Indians go to jail because they cannot afford to pay fines than whites do, the system of justice and the courts must share some of the blame for these shocking statistics.

Lawyers who fly on legal aid assignments into the northern areas of Saskatchewan for the monthly court tell of cases where native people who know they are not guilty of an offence decide to plead guilty anyway because it will make their lives easier in the future. When questioned about why they want to plead guilty, knowing full well they are not, they reply "We have to live here; you don't." The whole province north of a line from Meadow Lake to Prince Albert is without a single resident lawyer, so cases must be handled by outside lawyers who fly in once a month for the regular court sessions.

One case illustrating the arbitrary power of the RCMP over relatively powerless people is known in northern Saskatchewan communities as the La Loche lock-up. La Loche is a predominately native community in northern Saskatchewan, made up largely of Non-status Indians of Chippewayan descent. There is no TV so the main entertainments of the community are the weekly movie and the monthly court attended by white officials from the south. Estimates of the number of people on welfare run as high as 80 percent in the summer and up to half the population may be on probation at any given time. Liquor plays a key role in the lives of the people. Charges of bootlegging average about five per month; charges of drunkenness, about ten per month. On August 22, 1972, an intensely hot day, the RCMP arrested eleven Indian men on charges of drunkenness, locked them in two small cells, and detained them from 12:30 P.M. to 4 P.M. They also closed the windows of the cells, turned up the heat and refused water to the occupants. As a result of a letter to Attorney-General Roy Romanow from the Metis Society of Saskatchewan, through the Saskatoon Legal Aid Assistance Clinic, protesting the actions of the RCMP, the attorney-general's department launched an investigation. On December 4, 1972, Ned Shillington on behalf of Attorney-General Romanow informed the Saskatoon Legal Aid Assistance Clinic that no charges would be laid in connection with the incident, and that the actions of the RCMP under the circumstances were "justified." According to the investigation undertaken by the department, the following had been revealed: Yes, the windows were closed; they were closed because the locked-up men were "yelling profanities and obsenities, not fit to be heard by women and children." People familiar with the real life situation and the role of the RCMP in that situation, in La Loche find it a joke that such genteel, middle-class sensitivity about protecting women and children from abusive language could have been applied in this instance. All members of the RCMP deny that the heat was turned up. They say instead that the circulating fans were turned on, and that the extreme heat was caused by the large number of people in the small space as well as by the high temperature outside. They say that the "misunderstanding" about the heat being turned up was caused by the fact that the switch for the heater is close to the switch for the circulatory fans, and so the occupants may have thought the heater was being turned on rather than the fans when they saw Corporal Harrison turn on the fan switch. It is still difficult to imagine how the occupants could have been confused about the difference between air from a fan and hot air. Members of the RCMP admit that the occupants were refused water. Corporal Harrison gave the order. But they claim the reason for the refusal was that the men threatened to, and did, throw a pail of urine on the guard. Allegations of brutality during the arrests were dismissed as necessary force required for people "resisting arrest." The letter of explanation and the incident ended with the Attorney-General's representative saying, "In my opinion the action of the RCMP was justified." When asked in an interview by one of the authors in February 1973 about the incident, Mr. Romanow said, "I would probably not have used the phrase 'justified', had I written the letter myself." He went on to say that in investigations such as this one it is necessary to determine two things: Can a criminal charge be laid? And, can it be proven in court? "If these two conditions are not met it is not possible for us to take action against the RCMP," he said. Although no criminal action was possible, he said, he had brought the matter to the attention of the Assistant Commissioner of the RCMP and perhaps some internal disciplinary action resulted. He did not know.

Another area in northern Saskatchewan where there has been a great deal of friction between native people and the RCMP is Sandy Bay, a very depressed region with a population of between 600 and 700. A petition to Attorney-General Romanow and a number of signed statements by residents of the area alleging police brutality in the form of arm twisting, choking, and throwing people around, in the spring of 1972, resulted in another investigation by the Attorney-General's department. Sandy Bay at that time was policed from Pelican Narrows, 44 miles away, so officers were known to appear only during periods of difficulty. The incidents causing the residents to demand an investigation occurred when two officers arrested 22 people in one day on charges of drunkenness. One of these was an elderly woman, arrested close to her home. Residents of the community were most incensed of all by her arrest. The investigators' report said that the police, who in general had been over-zealous in arresting people on charges of drunkenness, had in that particular instance "exercised bad judgement" because of the animosity it created in the community. In commenting on the investigation, Mr. Romanow said, "There was some justification for complaint made by the population." However, the committee recommended as usual that no charges be laid. Full-time police service involving personnel other than those presently policing the area was urged in the report. The investigation revealed that "policy initiated by the P. A. Subdivision of the RCMP, of rigid and aggressive endorcement of Provincial Statutes, particularly the Liquor Act, has not reduced the problem of law enforcement but increased it."[11] The investigating committee recommended that this policy be abandoned and that "enforcement of Provincial Statutes be left to the discretion of members stationed at Sandy Bay based on their knowledge of the community."[12] Characteristically and in keeping with protecting the image of the Force, a spokesman for the Prince Albert division of the RCMP, responsible for policing the Sandy Bay area, denied any knowledge of incidents that may have taken place between members of the RCMP and the Indian and Metis community.[13]

On January 13, 1973, the Metis Society of Saskatchewan charged that RCMP members were committing sexual offences against young native women and cited one case which resulted in the dismissal of an officer. A 26-year-old treaty Indian woman (whose name is withheld because of the psychological damage she suffered as a result of the incident and its being made public) was apprehended by an officer of the RCMP in the lobby of the Alberta Hotel in Lloydminster, Alberta, and taken to the RCMP station, where she was advised that she would be charged for loitering on the hotel premises. The officer who apprehended her searched her, fondled her breasts, and advised her that she would be locked up overnight unless she submitted to his advances.

Thereupon she walked into the cell to stay overnight, but was brought out, grabbed by her hair, forced to her knees, and compelled to remain in that position while he removed his penis and forced it into her mouth. She was then released from custody and told to stay off the streets. She complained to her common-law husband and later consulted a lawyer in Lloydminster. Her complaint was investigated by two officers of the RCMP from North Battleford and Lloydminster who advised her that she would be subjected to a lie detector test. She then complained to a Catholic priest who brought the incident to the attention of the Saskatchewan Metis Society.[14]

The officer, Constable Allen Howard, was charged with indecent assault, and pleaded guilty to the charge on June 9, 1972, before Judge Policha at North Battleford. Mr. Norman Millar, agent for the Saskatchewan Attorney-General's Department in North Battleford, acted on behalf of the Crown. The officer was dismissed from the Force and fined $1,000 (with six months to pay). He moved out of the province. The young woman now lives in an isolated shack in the bushlands of

Saskatchewan, embarrassed to see many of her previous friends and acquaintances as a result of the incident. The Metis Society has its lawyer investigating, under the Criminal Injuries Compensation Act, compensation for the mental damage to the young woman resulting from the incident.

On June 20, 1972, Myron A. Kuziak, lawyer for the Metis Society and the complainant, wrote Attorney-General Romanow asking that the Crown appeal the sentence given the officer.

> Both ⌈name of woman⌉ and the Society are extremely concerned about the minor nature of the sentence in view of the serious nature of the crime, the fact that it was an RCMP officer who committed it while purporting to be carrying out his duties, and the certain knowledge that an Indian or Metis who was convicted of such a crime against a white woman would have received a jail sentence of considerable length, even on a first offence.
>
> We would suggest that the course of justice would be served by an appeal and by the Court of Appeal imposing a proper sentence. The community's standards, expectations and its right to protection from this kind of arrogant and racist behaviour are important matters for consideration by the Courts which should outweigh the inconvenience and hardship which would be placed upon the ex-Mountie by being brought back to be more properly dealt with. It is important that the Indian and Metis community in the Province know that their members cannot be criminally mistreated with relative impunity.
>
> Just to highlight the extreme laxity of the sentence I can advise that Judge Policha gave Mr. Howard six months time to pay the fine levied against him. As you know very few Metis or Indians would be allowed such a lengthy privilege.[15]

Attorney-General Romanow responded on July 4, 1972, and forwarded a report from Mr. Serge Kujawa, director of public prosecutions, which states:

> I am clearly unhappy with the sentence passed by Judge Policha. I do not think that a fine is an appropriate penalty for an indecent assault of this kind especially by someone taking advantage of his official position and victimizing a

person, not only with no position, but the disadvantage of being a frightened Indian.

The report goes on to argue that, although the sentence was not appropriate to the gravity of the crime committed, an appeal against the sentence would probably not be successful because it would be difficult to convince the court that the judge misdirected himself since he took into consideration all of the usual things.

> ...A rather important consideration in passing sentence herein is one that the Court of Appeal is aware of as well and although it is not expressed, the realization is there that if Constable Howard was sentenced to an institution, it would probably require solitary confinement to keep him from being badly beaten and perhaps killed. The unwritten rules in these institutions call for a "rape" to be "filled in". Another such rule is that a policeman, convicted of an offence, is to be punished. When you combine the two and consider the Indian involvement in the offence, plus the Indian population in the institutions, it is safe to say that imprisonment in this case would be far different from ordinary imprisonment. I have no doubt that this consideration weighed extremely heavily with Judge Policha and would with the Court of Appeal.
> ... I come to the above conclusion quite reluctantly because I still personally consider the sentence inadequate as not fitting the crime and I am sympathetic with the people who express a similar opinion. However, the people who express this opinion and ask for an appeal, are not aware of the difficulties to be encountered by the Crown in an appeal of this kind and I suggest we have no alternative but to inform them that we cannot appeal because we have no chance of success on the appeal. It would, of course be easier to launch the appeal and let the Court decision speak for itself but I would suggest that it would be an abdication of our responsibilities to the public as a whole.[16]

Although Mr. Kujawa is no doubt correct in his assessment that an appeal of the sentence would be an uphill battle and unlikely of success, the Indians and Metis of the province, quite justifiably, see this case as yet another evidence of gross injustice at their expense.

Although incidents as bizarre as the one cited above are not common, spokesmen for the Metis Society say that they know of other cases of sexual molestations of young Indian women while in the cutody of the RCMP and that the pattern of releasing them without charge is common. Jim Sinclair, president of the society, said, "These things happen. Young girls tell us of many similar offences but they are afraid to testify because of what may happen to them."[17] The blatant racist assumptions underlying such incidents are also common. After all, if this had happened to a white woman, would a lie detector test have been suggested by the officers investigating? Or would the officer have gotten away with a $1,000 fine and six months to pay?

Many aspects of life among native people are stark and brutal, and so liquor naturally plays a key role in most isolated northern communities — both socially and in terms of the power of the RCMP over people in those regions. One section of the Liquor Act in Saskatchewan is particularly significant in that it gives an officer a great deal of leeway as to its enforcement or non-enforcement and consequently a great deal of power over the people with whom he deals. After a conviction for bootlegging under the Liquor Act the house occupied or partly occupied by the convicted person "shall cease to be a dwelling house within the meaning of this Act during the time the person so convicted occupies the said house or any part thereof unless the convicting justice, or upon application to him any provincial magistrate, in his discretion otherwise declares."[18] In view of the fact that bootlegging convictions are numerous, that there are frequently many people living in one dwelling, and that it takes only one conviction for an entire dwelling to be declared out of bounds according to the Liquor Act, officers can exercise considerable leeway in how they enforce the law. Many of them choose to close their eyes to the fact that a particular house is not a "dwelling" within the meaning of the Act, because they prefer to have people drinking in a house rather than in a car or elsewhere. Others however, use the power the act gives them in a completely arbitrary and senseless manner as was evident in a case in October 1972 involving a 19-year-old Indian girl who lived in a small two-room house with her mother, father, brother and seven children. The night after her conviction on a charge of bootlegging, the RCMP broke open the door, searched the house and, finding a half-bottle of liquor in the cupboard, charged all four adult occupants with "having liquor in a place other than a dwelling." Theorectically, of course, they were guilty of an offence, but what's the point of charging these people under the circumstances? All it does is build up resentment towards the police. In no way does it touch on the fundamental problems responsible for alcoholism, which has reached serious proportions on many reserves.

To mention one more evidence of the power of the RCMP over northern people, in some communities members of the Force, acting as justices of the peace, sit on bail applications, sometimes in cases where they have provided the evidence for the original convictions.

The gravity of the problems between the RCMP and native communities is to a large extent the result of a racist attitude on the part of the police. As Dr. Howard Adams, a spokesman for the Metis Society has observed on many occasions the RCMP have been "brutal and oppressive" to native people. Today members of the Force often regard an assignment to an isolated northern community as a "punishment" assignment; consequently they go to these communities with a chip on their shoulder which in many cases results in their brutalizing and oppressing the people they are there to protect. In addition the RCMP are expected to enforce laws which are sometimes quite inappropriate to the northern situation. Recognizing that many problems exist in the North, Saskatchewan's Attorney-General Roy Romanow has mandated a member of his department to prepare a set of guidelines for RCMP operations in northern communities. However, as long as police policy is made in Ottawa, there will be no democracy as far as the local authorities are concerned. As long as the Force remains structured on totalitarian lines, it is doubtful if a more democratic operation is possible.

Certainly as long as there is a trace of racist policy which exploits and keeps Indian people in a state of subjugation, the police will continue to act as a colonial force. For police are in a sense just the instruments of racist oppression in the North in much the same way as they are the instruments of class oppression in labour disputes.

Chapter 11
The Fred Quilt case

On Sunday, November 28, 1971, Fred Quilt, a 55-year-old Chilcotin Indian, and his wife Christine drove in their pickup truck from their home on the Stone Reserve in the interior of British Columbia to the Anahim Reserve to attend a funeral. When they started back home late that afternoon they had in the truck with them their adopted son Robin, and Agnes Quilt, Fred's sister-in-law. They had been drinking vanilla extract and Fred, who was driving, turned in the wrong direction on Highway 20.

Meanwhile five miles away in Alexis Creek, RCMP constables Daryl Bakewell and Peter Eakins were having dinner at Eakins' home when they received a call from Corporal John Hest. He told them to check out a stalled pickup truck that was blocking the Chilcotin Highway about five miles east of Alexis Creek. Public health nurse Leslie Roberts had just seen it there and reported it to Corporal Hest.

When the constables got to the truck about 6 P.M., the Quilts were all asleep in it. Christine Quilt later testified that she remembered waking up and seeing a policeman by the truck. She said her husband was still asleep in the driver's seat next to her. Agnes was on the other side of her and Robin on the far passenger side.

Constable Eakins, senior constable at the Alexis Creek detachment of the RCMP, went to the driver's side of the truck and opened the door. According to his testimony, he asked the driver, who was sitting upright behind the wheel, to get out but there was no response. He said, "I noted the smell of vanilla coming from the vehicle and it appeared the driver was intoxicated." He then pulled Fred Quilt out of the truck, and he fell to the ground. In describing the manner of pulling Quilt from the truck, Eakins said, "The man's whole weight came down on him and Quilt fell on to the roadway. I believe it was his upper left side and shoulder." Eakins then told Bakewell to put Quilt in the police vehicle and went around to the passenger side of the pickup.

It was at this point, Christine Quilt testified later under oath through an interpreter, that she saw the constable — identified elsewhere as Daryl Bakewell, dressed in a yellow jacket and cowboy boots and so easily distinguishable from Eakins, who was in uniform — jump with both boots on her husband "quite a few times," saying "Get up you son of a bitch." Agnes Quilt also testified that she saw Bakewell jump up and down on her brother-in-law and heard him say the same thing.

Eakins denied that Bakewell jumped on Quilt. "I certainly would have heard it and I did not." During cross-examination Lawyer Harry Rankin, representing the Quilt family, pointed out that there was a "complete and absolute conflict in the evidence" of what happened after the two policemen arrived at the truck. He said, "There is no question of somebody being in doubt; someone is lying on their oath because Christine and Agnes Quilt say he [Bakewell] jumped up and down on the body of Fred Quilt."

He then asked Eakins, "Did you see any such thing happen?"

Eakins: No sir, I did not.
Rankin: Were you in a position to see it if it did happen?
Eakins: I don't think so.
Rankin: In other words it could have happened, you could have been in a position not to see it?
Eakins: I certainly would have heard it and I did not.

According to Bakewell's testimony at the second inquest, Quilt fell once more "face down" on his way to the police vehicle, as Bakewell "half-pushed and half-carried him."

After talking to the driver of another vehicle who stopped at the scene, Bakewell said he searched the cab of the Quilt truck and found three full bottles of vanilla extract, one half-full bottle, and one empty bottle. "I took all the bottles to the side of the road and broke them on the rocks . . . it was the simplest solution." He said there was no legal justification for breaking the bottles but that the RCMP make a general practice of it, because if the vanilla "was returned to the occupants or ended up on the reserve, future problems would develop."

In his testimony Bakewell denied having jumped up and down on Quilt or having "put the boots to him." He identified a pair of Western boots produced at the inquest as the pair he was wearing on November 28. According to RCMP testimony, the boots were not sent to a crime lab for analysis of possible fibres on them because the RCMP had been unaware of any allegation that Constable Bakewell had used the boots on Fred Quilt.

During examination by Lawyer Castillou, appearing on behalf of the estate of the deceased in the first inquest, Bakewell said that he may have used the phrase "Get up you son of a bitch."

Castillou: You are saying, officer, you may have said, "Get up you son of a bitch"?

Bakewell: I may have said a lot of things.

Castillou: Could you have said that?

Bakewell: Yes, I could have.

Castillou: You certainly would have remembered if you had said it, if you want to make such a statement?

Bakewell: No, sir.

Castillou: Why not?

Bakewell: That does not strike me as being particularly noteworthy.

Under questioning from Lawyer Rankin during the second inquest, Bakewell said he probably spoke to Quilt, and added: "It would be equivalent to speaking to a small child, telling him to do something. You just don't remember it, at least I don't.

When asked by Lawyer Rankin, "Was there an allegation made against you at Chase involving the beating of an Indian boy?", Bakewell's response was, "It was never brought to my attention."

When asked by Rankin if he was angry at being called out that evening, Bakewell denied it but admitted he was perhaps annoyed to a minor degree.

During the second inquest, Eakins said there was no key in the ignition at the time of the incident and the hood of the truck was cold to the touch. "As a result I determined there would be insufficient evidence to arrest this person on a charge of having care and control of a motor vehicle while impaired.

Eakins said he told the other three occupants — Christine, Agnes and Robin Quilt to step out of the pickup, and get in the rear seat of the police vehicle with Fred Quilt.

Constables Eakins and Bakewell then tried to push the Quilt truck to the shoulder of the road so it would not block traffic.

They were able to push it only about two feet. Constable Eakins tried to shift the gear, but it appeared to be jammed. Although the pickup was still blocking one lane of the highway, there seemed to be enough room for other traffic to get by, so Eakins and Bakewell went back to the police vehicle and Eakins drove the Quilts back to the Anahim Reserve, about a mile and a half away, despite the fact that their home was on the Stone Reserve.

According to the Quilts' testimony, Fred was moaning in pain. At the reserve, Constable Eakins let them off under a street light and watched them walk "about 75 yards towards the reserve church." According to Eakins, "They were staggering quite obviously." According to the Quilts' Fred could barely walk when the RCMP dropped them off at Anahim; blood was running down his face and on to his shirt from a cut on his head.

On their way back to Alexis Creek, Constable Eakins testified, the constables came upon the Quilt truck again and realizing it was still a hazard on the road, stopped to put highway flares 10 feet in front and 10 feet behind the pickup. Then they drove back to Alexis Creek for a tow cable. The police vehicle was supposed to be equipped with a tow cable, but it had been used a few days previously on another vehicle and left in the police office. The winch had jammed a week earlier too, Eakins said.

When Eakins and Bakewell returned with the cable, according to their testimony, they found the Quilt truck on fire. It had been pushed over an embankment and was about 30 or 35 yards from where they had left it.

Meanwhile, according to the Quilts, Percy Jeff's two daughters took Fred Quilt into their home, where he sat by the fire groaning in pain. Christine Quilt went immediately with Raymond Stump to fetch the Quilt truck. They found it in flames off to the side of the road. They said they found the red wrapping from a used flare near the burning truck, and Christine alleged that the RCMP had set fire to the truck.

Eakins testified that he did not know what became of the flares he had left at the scene. He said there had been an investigation into what became of them, but they were never recovered.

When Eakins got back to Alexis Creek, his wife gave him a message to phone Christine Quilt at a house on the Anahim Reserve. Christine told him the truck had been pushed over the bank and set on fire. "I said I was aware of this and it would be looked into," he said.

At about 7 P.M., Mary Billy went to get Sister Jeanita Cormier, who had just moved to the Anahim Reserve, and Fred Quilt told the nursing sister that a policeman had kicked him on the side and that he was in extreme pain. Sister Jeanita gave him some 292's and put an elastic bandage around his ribs. She then phoned the RCMP to tell them that she suspected Fred Quilt had broken ribs and should be taken to a hospital. In his testimony, Constable Eakins said Sister Jeanita Cormier had phoned to say that "a Patrick Quilt had some broken ribs" and she wished him to go to the hospital the next day. At the time, Constable Eakins did not make any connection between this phone call and the stalled pickup truck.

After speaking with the RCMP, Christine Quilt and Geneva Sam, a Chilcotin-English interpreter, walked almost a mile through the snow to call on Father O'Brien, and Oblate priest in the area. Through the interpreter, Christine asked Father O'Brien to phone the provincial court judge in nearby Redstone, Tim Bayliff. Father O'Brien tried to reach Bayliff that evening and again in the morning but was unable to get hold of him. Father O'Brien was not asked to testify at the first inquest, but he later submitted a report telling what he had heard on the evening of the 28th. According to the RCMP, he was not asked to testify because they did not realize that he had anything to say.

After visiting Father O'Brien, Christine Quilt returned to Percy Jeff's house to find her husband still in severe pain. About midnight she went to Sister Jeanita again and got some sleeping pills for him. Later she phoned to the nurses' residence in Alexis Creek and asked a nurse to come and see her husband.

The next day, Monday, November 29, around 10:30 A.M. public health nurse Leslie Roberts went to see the injured man. Fred told Miss Roberts the RCMP had beat him up. The nurse made arrangements for an ambulance to pick Fred up. A Doctor Dormaar also visited the injured man, gave him a brief examination, and phoned for an ambulance.

At 6 o'clock that evening the ambulance came for Fred Quilt, who by then had been in serious pain for over 24 hours. In the ambulance however, was the body of a dead child, and since the Chilcotins believe that if someone travels with a dead person he will be the next to die, Fred did not go with the ambulance. When Sister Jeanita heard that Fred had not gone in the ambulance, she tried to arrange for it to come again the following day.

On the morning of Tuesday, November 30, Lawrence Stump drove Fred Quilt, very slowly because he was in pain, to the Stone Reserve, a distance of 15 miles. In response to a call from Dr. Han Chou Lee in Williams Lake, an ambulance arrived at the Quilt home around one that afternoon and drove Fred Quilt to Williams Lake, 75 miles away. They had to give him oxygen on the way to keep him breathing. The ambulance arrived at the Cariboo Memorial Hospital at 3 P.M. They took x-rays of the sick man, but before Dr. Lee could complete his examination Fred Quilt died. The time of his death was 4:20. Christine Quilt first heard the news of her husband's death over the radio the next day.

Dr. Lee performed an autopsy on the evening of November 30, under the supervision of Coroner Sidney S. Leitch. Constable de Bruijn of the Williams Lake RCMP was also present. The autopsy showed a complete transection pulmonar portion of the small bowel, which casued general peritonitis, an inflammation of the covering of the organs of the abdominal cavity. The transection in the small bowel could have been caused only by a trauma, i.e., a strong external force. Dr. Lee estimated that Fred Quilt received the fatal injury about 48 hours before his death. There were no bruises or cuts on the body. The doctor also stated that surgery within about 12 hours of the injury could have saved the man's life.

RCMP officer Robert Holland took several pictures of the body of Fred Quilt at the time of the autopsy.

A coroner's inquest was ordered on the evening of Fred Quilt's death, and six jurors were picked the same night. The Williams Lake detachment of the RCMP, under the direction of Coroner S. S. Leith, an ex-RCMP officer, selected the jury which was all white.

The first inquest into when, how and after what manner Fred Quilt came to his death was held in Williams Lake on January 13, 14 and 15, 1972 before Coroner S. S. Leith, with 24 witnesses giving testimony.

The "estate of Fred Quilt" was represented by Henry Castillou. The courtroom was a confusing and alienating experience for some of the Indian witnesses. There was also a language problem, because Christine Quilt, the main witness, had to give her testimony through an English-Chilcotin interpreter.

After hearing evidence and deliberating for three hours, the jury returned the following verdict:

> That Frederick Quilt of Stone Reserve, aged 55 years, died on the 30th of November A.D., 1972, as a result of peritonitis. We find this death was unnatural and that it was accidental. We attach no blame to any person in connection with the death. We recommend that assistance be provided to minority ethnic groups as to their rights pertaining to the law and obligations in giving testimony.

The verdict of "Death — unnatural and accidental" with "no blame" attached to any person was greeted with storms of protest from Indian leaders and organizations, labor leaders and unions, church groups, service clubs, political parties and individuals.

On December 17, Tony Belcourt of the Native Council of Canada, Fred House from British Columbia Association of Non-Status Indians (B.C.A.N.S.I.) and Clarence Dennis of the Union of British Columbia Indian Chiefs (UBCIC) went to Ottawa to discuss the circumstances of Fred Quilt's death with the then Minister of Justice John Turner and Solicitor-General Jean-Pierre Goyer. Both promised to look into the matter.

In February the Fred Quilt Committee was formed for the purpose of publicizing the injustices of the case. As soon as the 438-page transcript of the inquest became available, the committee purchased a copy and went after legal advice. Lawyers Harry Rankin and Bill Deverell advised the committee that the transcript contained sufficient evidence in it to charge constable Bakewell with manslaughter and advised them to proceed with a civil case against the RCMP. The central demand of the Fred Quilt Committee, therefore, was that the attorney-general lay charges against Constable Bakewell.

After considerable pressure, the B.C. Attorney-General Leslie Peterson ordered B. C. Chief Coroner Glen McDonald to review the evidence presented at the inquest and to take new evidence. According to the Fred Quilt Committee, the new investigation ordered by Peterson was "a secret investigation to be conducted by a special, secret investigator who just happened to be a policeman."[1] The new investigation was totally unacceptable to the committee, who pointed out:

It was RCMP who "allegedly" beat Fred Quilt. It was an ex-RCMP officer who ordered the autopsy and conducted the first inquest. RCMP chose the jurors. RCMP supoenaed witnesses. Two RCMP did the first investigation of the case and now again it's two police doing the secret special investigation.[2]

The B.C. Supreme Court quashed the inquest held at Williams Lake in January on the grounds that there was an association between two members of that jury and the RCMP, and ordered a second inquest for July 1972.

During the second inquest Christine Quilt again alleged that the RCMP had used one of the flares to set fire to the truck, but Judge McNeil ruled this ineligible as evidence since she did not see it happen. RCMP Corporal Robert Holland, of the identification section of the RCMP at Williams Lake, testified that he first looked at the Quilt truck on December 3, 1971, and that at that time he knew that there was an allegation that an assault had taken place. Under questioning from Harry Rankin, he said that for the truck to get from where it had been on the road down a bank to the place where it was later found 30 to 35 yards away, it would have had to be pushed either by manpower or another vehicle. He agreed that the truck could not have set fire to itself, and that the occurence had some of the elements of the crime of damage to property connected with it.

Asked why, in view of Quilt's death and these circumstances, he did not order the truck to be towed away to Alexis Creek and impounded for scientific work on the reason for the fire, Holland said he did not feel that was his responsibility.

Rankin: Whose responsibility it it?
Holland: The investigating member.

Holland said at that time this would have been Hest's responsibility. He also said that it had never crossed his mind to have the truck towed in and added, "a burned out truck is a burned out truck."

Rankin: Here there was a death in which there was an allegation of a stomping or kicking so there was something more than a burned out truck.
Holland: You are correct.

The burning of the truck remains one of the unsolved mysteries of the Fred Quilt case.

Conflicting medical evidence arose at the second inquest over whether or not a complete transection of the small bowel in the area indicated by Dr. Lee could have taken place. Dr. John Sturdy, a pathologist from New Westminster, said that he had never seen a transection without injury to other organs as well. He also said that sections for microscopic examination should have been taken. Dr. Lee testified earlier that his examination was with the naked eye only, on the instructions of Williams Lake Coroner S. S. Leith. Dr. Sturdy said he believed Dr. Lee broke the bowel in some way during the autopsy, "completely inadvertently and honestly," and should have looked for some other cause of the peritonitis.

On cross-examination by Lawyer Rankin, Dr. Sturdy said it would be "essential, almost mandatory" for the Williams Lake coroner to direct a thorough investigation in the autopsy because of the suggestion Quilt had been jumped on by someone. On further questioning from Rankin, Dr. Sturdy said that he personally found it hard to accept that an RCMP officer would jump up and down on an Indian.

After a marathon inquest lasting three weeks, the jury gave its verdict on August 3. It reads in full:

We find the death was caused by general peritonitis of the abdomen over a 48-hour period, caused by a perforation of the small bowel. The perforation was the result of an injury by way of an unknown blunt force applied by an unknown object to the lower right abdomen.

The injury was sustained between the time Quilt was removed from the Quilt's vehicle and assisted to the police vehicle on the Chilcotin Road on November 28.

Due to unwillingness of Quilt to avail himself of ambulance service and medical attention that was made available to him, Quilt's activities during this period of time, the modes of transportation, the conditions of the road and the lapse of time were contributing factors.

The recommendations of the jury included a directive to all law-enforcement agencies to exercise more care and attention in their handling of people. The jury said it believed there was reason to question the handling of individuals by law-enforcement agencies. The jury also recommended a more extensive court worker program, because most native Indians are uninformed of their legal rights and the legal aid available to them. They also called for a full investigation of medical services in the Chilcotin area by the federal Department of Health and Welfare with the results of such investigation being implemented.

The verdict of the second inquest brought renewed demands by the Fred Quilt Committee that a charge be laid in the death of Fred Quilt since death was the result of an injury sustained while he was being handled by the police. The committee wanted a judge and jury to deal with Bakewell in the same way they would deal with any other citizen against whom similar sworn allegations had been made.

Lawyer Harry Rankin, too, in commenting on the case, said that in his view there was enough evidence to place Bakewell on trial: "If one person swears on oath he saw another person injuring someone, and that someone dies, that is sufficient evidence for a trial.[3] He added that it does not mean there is sufficient evidence for a conviction.

The Native Council of Canada, which represents non-status Indians and Metis, said the fact that there was a second inquest into the death of a native Indian is an accomplishment in itself.

Dr. Howard Adams, a Saskatchewan Metis leader, said in commenting on the Quilt case:

What has happened to Fred Quilt is not new to the native people of Canada. Brothers and sisters die every day throughout the nation as a result of the brutal and vicious system of racism and its agents . . . We must do more than demand legal action. We should not bother ourselves with trying to improve the relationship between the native people and the Mounted Police for that is not a possibility. After all, the official duty of the police is to intimidate, control and keep us in our place. The mounties operate according to their stereotype images of us as savages.[4]

The Quilt case is one of the rare cases where documentation is available. As Frank Calder, the Indian MLA in the B.C. Legislature, said, "Quilt is only one case among many which shows that Indians are not getting justice.

Harry Rankin has said:

It would be a gross over-simplification to "explain" the death of Fred Quilt by concluding that he was the unfortunate victim of "bad" individuals or of an unfortunate set of circumstances, that he was allegedly beaten to death by a policeman, who, contrary to the general rule, happened to be brutal. To get at the cause of Fred Quilt's death requires not only the punishment of those immediately responsible, but tackling the whole system of racism as it exists against Indians in our province.[5]

The extent to which racist attitudes permeate the RCMP is relevant to all Canadians. Ex-corporal Jack Ramsay commented on it in his *Maclean's* expose when he said, "Of course, the easiest pinch for statistics is the Indian."

Ramsay also raises questions about the evidence RCMP officers give in court. He writes: "Especially during my last seven years on the force, I watched fellow members lying, falsifying records and ignoring suspects' rights until I came to dislike putting on the famous scarlet tunic, because it made me feel like a hypocrite." He further states that "any member with ten years' service has learned to lie skillfully." A member must place the force ahead of truth, justice, and service to the people of Canada . . . You lie, first to survive; then, as fear and guilt blunt conscience, to get ahead."[6]

Why are there so many unanswered questions in the Fred Quilt case? Who set fire to the Quilt truck? Why was the investigation of that fire inconclusive? Were Constable Bakewell's boots not taken for examination because the RCMP were unaware of the allegations of police brutality? If the injury that caused Quilt's death was sustained between the time Quilt was removed from the Quilt vehicle and the time he was assisted into the police vehicle, as the jury in the second inquest found, why wasn't an investigation made and additional charges laid?

Chapter 12
The Muskego affair

On October 10, 1970, four juveniles ran away from the Saskatchewan Boys' School in Regina. They stole a volkswagon and drove it out of town where the car's motor seized and they abandoned it. A mile and a half farther on, they found a 1968 Ford in a farmer's garage "hotwired" it and took off again. Their original plan was to go to Melfort but Michael Muskego, who was driving, took a wrong turn and they ended up on the road to Saskatoon, a widely-travelled, paved highway, four lanes wide part of the way.

What the boys didn't know was that on the previous day, two RCMP officers had been shot to death in the MacDowall district of Saskatchewan, allegedly by one Wilfred Stanley Robertson, so there were a large number of police patrols out. In fact, the search for Robertson was one of the biggest manhunts in Saskatchewan's history. Every newscast was full of it.

The farmer reported the theft of his car in the early morning hours of October 10, and soon Constable Gordon Michael Bickerton of the RCMP spotted it in the Chamberlain district, travelling north. Bickerton was travelling south at the time, but he turned around and followed the Ford. According to his testimony later the youths were travelling at about 65 or 70 miles per hour when he spotted them. In the town of Chamberlain, they slowed down to 15 or 20, and he was able to get close enough to read the licence number in order to be sure that this was the vehicle the police were looking for. He contacted the RCMP radio room in Regina and activated the red dome light on his police car in an effort to stop the other vehicle. It was still dark, approximately 6:20 A.M.

Seeing the red flashing light of the RCMP vehicle, the youths accelerated up to 90 or 100 miles per hour. Constable Bickerton chased them to the town of Davidson, where Chief Constable Gray of the Davidson City Police, a former member of the RCMP set up a roadblock. The youths managed to get around it. Both Constable Bickerton and Chief Constable

Gray pursued them north another five miles. There Constable Bickerton dropped out, but Chief Constable Gray continued, on through the town of Bladworth at a speed of 100 miles per hour, even at times reaching his maximum speed of 130 miles per hour. At Kenaston the two cars passed another RCMP car parked on the side of the road. At Hanley the police had set up another roadblock, this time by putting a transport across the highway. The car Michael Muskego was driving went around the transport to the right and continued on its way. At that point Constable Fairbridge joined the chase, and approximately five miles south of Saskatoon Staff Sergeant Edmondson joined in an unmarked car. There were now two Mounted Police cars, the Davidson Town Police car and Staff Sergeant Edmondson's car behind the stolen car. Staff Sergeant Edmondson testified that he got up to about 85 or 90 miles per hour and then dropped back. "I just didn't see how it could keep up." He also advised the others over the radio that there were only four young people in the car and told them to use caution. His advice was not heeded by the other members of the Force, although they heard his radio message to "Cool it; it's only a bunch of kids."

Two of the juveniles testifying at the coroner's inquest said that when they saw the last roadblock outside Saskatoon, they told Michael to stop because they didn't think they could get through it, but he replied that he would "rather go to the hospital than go to jail." One of them explained that during the chase, when they asked him to slow down or stop, "he said that he didn't want to stop because he didn't want to get beat up." Another said, "I was talking to him for a while but he said he didn't want to get beat up, like he said when he was at Onion Lake he got beat up by the Mounties there."

Now a third roadblock was set up, and two RCMP officers with .308 calibre rifles, stood beside it. As the car driven by Muskego approached and appeared to be attempting to go around the roadblock, one of the RCMP officers fired from close range. The bullet went through the side of the car near the driver's door. The car went out of control and turned end over end. When they removed Muskego from the car moments later, he was dead. Nobody else was seriously injured.

Micheal John Muskego came from a large Indian family. Before being sent to the Saskatchewan Boys' School, he had finished grade six at the Indian School on the Onion Lake Reserve. At the time of his death, he was 15 years old.

Later, in the morgue at St. Paul's Hospital in Saskatoon, Dr. Harry Emson examined the body and discovered a bullet hole in the chest of the 15-year-old boy. Up to this time the police had not mentioned firearms.

After Dr. Emson informed the police of his findings a series of conflicting reports began to appear in the Saskatoon *Star-Phoenix* and the Regina *Leader Post*. The first public acknowledgement that the boy had been shot appeared in the *Star-Phoenix* on October 14, with quotes from an afficial statement released by the RCMP. The Saskatoon detachment said that firearms had been used, but had not been reported because the officers had had to leave the scene at once to go in search of Wilfred Stanley Robertson in the MacDowall area and so could not wait to file a report of the fatal shooting of the driver of the car. They also said that the police had been under the impression that the driver might have been Wilfred Stanley Robertson himself, which was the real reason they were taking no chances. In a story in the October 16 *Leader Post*, Assistant Commissioner J. L. Vachon of the RCMP denied any connection between the hunt for Robertson and the killing of Muskego. "At no time was it felt that the vehicle driven by Michael John Muskego, might in fact contain Robertson, nor was it the reason a shot was fired at the vehicle," he said. However, no other reason for a shot was given by Assistant Commissioner Vachon. The Saskatoon detachment then changed its story and acknowledged that they did in fact know that it was not Wilfred Stanley Robertson; but that they wanted to prevent this car, which was going at dangerous speed, from getting into the city of Saskatoon, where it might injure or kill someone.

NDP MPs John Burton (Regina East) and Lorne Nystrom (Yorkton-Melville) questioned Solicitor-General G. T. McIlraith in the House of Commons on October 20 about the conflicting reports and were assured by him that an investigation was being carried on into the Muskego shooting and the discrepancies in news reports would be included.

An inquest was ordered and convened on October 26, 1970. Under existing arrangements, a corner's jury is usually not picked by the coroner, but by the RCMP. The coroner's jury consists of six or more people who are usually picked from a roster of persons known to the RCMP.

In a later case in British Columbia, which also involved the death of an Indian — the Fred Quilt case — The Supreme

Court of Canada ruled that a coroner's jury selected by police officers and or which was composed of persons who were sympathetic to or might be sympathetic to the police was an improperly constituted jury. In that case — a year later than the Muskego case — a second inquest was ordered by the Supreme Court.

In this case, the foreman of the jury selected by the RCMP in Saskatoon was Norman Bennett, a retired RCMP officer. One of the other members was James Brook Wrigley, a justice of the peace who for a number of years had handled RCMP matters such as releasing prisoners on bail in the city of Saskatoon.

When the inquest convened on October 26, 1970, in the Court House in Saskatoon, R. D. R. Caldwell, the agent of the attorney-general at Saskatoon, appeared for the Crown, and Silas Halyk appeared on behalf of the RCMP, by special appointment from the Department of Justice at Ottawa. Mr. M. Irwin, a young solicitor in Saskatoon, appeared on behalf of the three surviving juveniles in the case, who were wards of the Saskatchewan government. The Coroner was Dr. Sydney Fogel, a man with no legal training, but who had held the position of coroner for some time. Assisting Mr. Caldwell in his examination was Sergeant Evanoff, a long-time member of the RCMP, whose job was to assist in the preparation of questions which would be submitted to the witnesses.

A critical reading of the transcript of the inquest raises some unanswered questions about the death of Michael Muskego. No one, throughout the entire inquest, asked such questions as "Why were shotguns not used instead of high-powered rifles, if the purpose was, as alleged, to shoot out the tires and not to shoot any occupants of the car?" The evidence disclosed that the shot was fired from a distance of about ten feet directly into the side of the car. The allegation that the officer was really aiming at the tires is immaterial if he was firing from that distance. Why did he not use one of the shotguns which were available on the spot, which would have been much better for blowing out a tire?

By the time of the inquest, the police were alleging that their purpose in shooting at all was to prevent the stolen car from getting into the city of Saskatoon, where it might have done serious damage at the high speed at which it was travelling. They admitted that any number of vehicles were available for a roadblock so that it would have been possible to block the road completely in order to prevent the Muskego car from going around. What they actually did was to leave a space in the roadblock big enough for a car to drive through. When Muskego attempted to drive through it, one of the officers fired from close range. The scene at which the shooting took place is on a level stretch of road, which at that point is a four-lane highway. The ditches at the sides are level, so a car could very easily go around any vehicle drawn across the road; therefore a roadblock at that point could not be very effective. About 100 yards north is an overpass over a set of railway tracks. At that point, there would be no difficulty whatsoever in blocking the roadway completely. Since a car could get by there only by crashing onto the railway tracks below, it would have been the logical place to set up the road block if the intention was to stop the car at any cost.

Constable Jerome Federowich testified that around 6:30 A.M. on October 10, he and Constable Bezzola of the Saskatoon detachment were ordered to the MacDowall district. Actually their job was to hunt for Wilfred Stanley Robertson and, if necessary, to shoot him. They were armed with shotguns and .308 rifles as well as revolvers. However, before going to MacDowall they were asked to assist on a roadblock just south of Saskatoon. Sergeant Evanoff was in charge of the undertaking at that point and Federowich was requested to wait near the overpass. When he got there, there was a white tanker across the north-bound lane approximately 250 feet south of the overpass, and there were other power units with trailers behind this unit. He asked the tanker to move up the road near the overpass and also requested two other semi-trailers to go into the south-bound lane and block it off right across from the tanker when it moved up. This would still enable the fleeing car to get by. He then went to the bridge, which is used by north-bound traffic, drew his revolver and waited there. He intended to fire at any vehicle that came his way, as he said at the inquest, "by shooting at the vehicle's tires or something like that."

He testified that he heard a bang but did not see anybody use any firearms, and then saw the Muskego vehicle go out of control and flip over on its roof. He rushed over to the car and assisted in removing the occupants.

The next witness was John Ayton Bezzola, a dark-haired young constable with an insignia on his arm indicating that he had qualified as a marksman. The agent of the attorney-general requested that Bezzola be given the protection of the Saskatchewan and Canada Evidence Acts, which would prevent him from being prosecuted as a result of any evidence that he might give. Bezzola stated that he held a Bachelor of Arts degree and a Professional Teaching Certificate and was in the process of completing his Bachelor of Education degree. He also indicated that he was proficient in the use of a rifle and hand-gun, having fired rifles as a hobby since his high school days.

Constable Bezzola stated that he had the police car radio on and could hear any transmissions concerning the state of the chase. He knew from the radio that the car had gone by several roadblocks by this time, at Davidson and Hanley. He received instructions from Sergeant Evanoff to set up a roadblock where the tanker and the two semi-trailers were presently in the north-bound lane just south of the overpass, so he and Federowich went back to that position immediately and told the driver of the tanker to park his truck further north towards the overpass and instructed the two semi-trailer drivers to drive north on the north-bound lane and cross over to the south-bound lane at their first opportunity and come back. When they had done that, Bezzola instructed them to set up immediately west of the tanker. All north and south bound lanes were then blocked by a semi-trailer or tanker. However, there is a wide centre median which is even enough for a car to drive on without tipping over. Two police cars were placed in the median area, one facing in an easterly direction and slightly angled to the north, the other on the west part of the median also facing in a north easterly direction. There was room left between the roadblock and the police cars, and the centre of the median was purposely left open. Both doors of one police car were open and the police radio was turned up as loud as it would go.

At this point in the inquest, it became clear that the agent of the attorney-general was phrasing his questions in such a way at to protect the police, particularly Constable Bezzola, from recriminations. The following questions and answers from his examination of Constable Bezzola demonstrate this:

Q. Now appreciating that I am sure this went by very quickly, did you consider the possibility of what might happen should the car indeed get around the last roadblock successfully?

A. Yes, that was my greatest concern, of course, the fact that we were the last roadblock and that possibly the final opportunity to stop this vehicle from entering the early morning rush hour traffic.

Q. And from what we have heard I take it the City proper is a matter of possibly a mile or two farther north until you are on Eighth Street East among other things?

A. Yes, the city limits I believe are approximately a mile north of our location there.

Q. And did you consider at about this point the possibility of firing at the car if it did not stop?

A. Yes, I contemplated firing at the radiator of the vehicle as it came up the incline towards me but discounted that because of the possibility of other things happening. The marked police car was immediately behind it as well as numerous cars and individuals were down at the roadblock at the Grasswood Esso intersection there and the possibilities of a richochet had to be considered.

Q. I take it you abandoned that idea, did you?

A. Yes, I didn't fire.

Q. What happened as the car got immediately close to the roadblock? What did it appear it was going to do?

A. He turned off the paved portion of the road and on to the dirt embankment and continued on the embankment as if to go around on the east side of the tanker trailer.

Q. Now, you, I take it, had been out and looked roughly at that embankment and situation there?

A. Yes, we had.

Q. And did it appear to you from what you have said that it would be possible to manoeuvre a car around there if the driver took enough care?

A. Yes, I don't know the angle of the slope but the police car went around it right immediately after the stolen vehicle and had no difficulty.

Q. I see, and you had seen the situation though, before the stolen car went around?

A. Yes.

Bezzola went on to describe how he fired allegedly at the front tire of the car as it went by him. He stated that the car was going about 90 miles an hour as it went down into the ditch and back up onto the roadway, and he fired at a right angle to it from a distance of about 12 to 15 feet as it went by him.

He said that when he went up to the car and found the driver dead, the thought occurred to him that the boy might have been hit by a bullet, but he examined the driver's door and saw no bullet hole. (Photographic evidence later showed a bullet hole clearly visible near the left front door.) He could not see any evidence of a bullet hole in the left front tire either, he said, although he did not search carefully. He agreed with Constable Federowich that the bullet must have entered the car from the front, which meant the car was drifting slightly sideways at the time he fired the bullet, although as far as he was concerned, he said, he was at right angles to it.

Possibly with a view toward creating a rationale for the use of firearms, an attempt was again made to establish an association between this incident and the MacDowall situation:

Caldwell: And in your mind when you set up and prepared and eventually did shoot at the car were you considering this thing in the light of the MacDowall situation or on its own merits so to speak, an isolated episode?

Bezzola: Well, nothing had been given to us in the way of information that the two incidents were not linked, however, we were treating it on its own merit, it seemed like something far more serious than a simple stolen vehicle.

Immediately after shooting, Bezzola and Federowich left the scene and went to MacDowall. Here is how Bezzola described that, under the skillful guidance of Mr. Caldwell:

Q. I take it there came a time when you and Federowich left about your original assignment and went on north, did you?

A. Yes, we had been detailed, like I mentioned previously, to meet Sergeant Head at MacDowall and we were already an hour late for that assignment, and we left the scene almost immediately.

Q. And by the time you left the scene had you any notion that the bullet had hit an occupant of the car?

A. No, I was unaware of that.

Q. Now, when did you learn of that?

A. It was late Sunday evening, the 11th of October.

Constable Johnston described the incident as follows:

Q. What happened then, Constable Johnston?

A. The '68 Ford was proceeding north at a high rate of speed and as it approached the semi-trailer where we were at, I noticed the vehicle start to cut into the ditch and I would estimate the speed to be approximately 90 to 100 miles an hour when it entered the ditch. It then proceeded through the ditch and at this time Constable Bezzola had the rifle up to his shoulder and he was pointing down more or less at an angle something like this, (indicating) and from my position it appeared as though he was aiming at the tire. I then had my rifle up to my shoulder as the vehicle continued by and was looking at it through the scope. This was a couple of seconds after it had already passed the semi-trailer.

Q. And what happened as you saw Bezzola pointing in this manner?

A. Well, I just saw him pointing. At that time I had the rifle up myself and all I could see was what was in the scope area and I heard what sounded like a shot.

One of the juveniles, who was sitting in the right-front passenger seat, testified as follows:

Q. Where were you sitting?

A. I was sitting by the door and —————* was sitting in the middle.

Q. There were only three of you in the front seat?

A. Yes.

Q. Now you say that the bullet hit your door.

A. I said a bullet smashed the window and I heard a noise.

Q. On Mickey's side the bullet smashed the window?

A. Yes.

Q. And then you heard a noise?

A. Yes, I heard a noise and it hit by my door.

Further questioning of the juvenile by Caldwell about the shot going through the window confirmed the original testimony.

* Under Section 12(3) of the Juvenile Delinquents Act, the names of juveniles who are involved in criminal matters are not to be published.

Q. Did you think it went through the window?

A. Yes.

Q. Why did you think that?

A. Well, because I was looking in the window and saw the glass broke.

Q. And this was when you were passing the roadblock, was it?

A. Yes.

The other youth who was sitting in the front seat, next to Muskego, also testified that he thought the shot went through the window.

I saw a guy standing there with a rifle or something and he shot. I thought it went through the window, I don't know — and Mike's arms went up and he fell on top of me.

Under cross-examination from Mr. Irwin, who asked him why he thought it went through the window, the youth said, "I just heard a funny noise which sounded like shattering glass."

The statements made by the youths two hours after the accident were never called for as evidence by the agent for the attorney-general or by anyone else. In his testimony Sergeant Evanoff indicated that a junior constable, Constable Somers, had been sent to Kilburn Hall, where two of the youths were being held, and to the hospital to take statements from the boys "in connection with where they got this car and things that involved the chase."

Sergeant Evanoff, who was second in command of the Saskatoon detachment, did not recall seeing anyone using firearms at the scene, although he was present and was in charge of the various personnel. He did not seem to know that any of the officers had taken their rifles out of the car, or that any of them had used rifles to stop the Muskego vehicle. As he said in answer to a question from Mr. Caldwell:

Q. And what was the first word you had that there was the possibility of a bullet wound?

A. Sometime after 10:30, and I would say 12:00 o'clock on the 10th I received a call from Dr. Fogel that the pathologist had indicated there was some possibility of bullets or bullet wounds in Muskego. And Dr. Fogel questioned me about the condition of the vehicle and whether or not there was any shots fired and I believe that I told him that "No sir, as far as I can recollect, most of us knew that these were youths in this car and that no shots had been fired."

At about 5:30 P.M., Sergeant Evanoff received a call at home from Staff Sergeant Waterman, who had reviewed the statements from the two boys at Kilburn Hall, which indicated that "there had been a *couple of shots* fire at them." Sergeant Evanoff noted to Staff Sergeant Waterman the possibility that "these youths were enlarging on their story," but said he would look into it when he returned to the office at a later time.

Sergeant Evanoff testified that later that day he went out to the Grasswood Esso service station, where the car was, examined it again, and indeed found a bullet hole in the "left front fender just ahead of the left front door." He also saw that there was loose glass in the car, that the windshield was cracked, and that the left front vent was shattered. (How did he fail to see these things in his first investigation? Nobody ever asked.) He then instructed that the car be taken in for further investigation.

During Sergeant Evanoff's testimony, the importance of the investigation being undertaken at MacDowall involving the death of two RCMP officers was again pointed out:

Caldwell: Now I take it that even at this stage the Mac-Dowall business would still be in full swing?

Evanoff: Yes, it was, sir.

Caldwell: And lots of personnel being moved around.

Evanoff: That's right, yes.

Caldwell: Was Constable Bezzola still involved at that time?

Evanoff: He was at the MacDowall area at this time.

Sargeant Evanoff testified that he knew that the occupants of the car were young boys.

Q. At what stage did you personally know there were youths in the car?

A. I had been following the chase as it were, from chamberlain and somewhere due south of us Staff Sergeant Edmondson had become involved in the chase and I would say when he was about two and one-half miles behind me this car had passed him in the median and re-entered the highway and came up behind him back on the highway and Staff Sergeant Edmondson had made some comment at this time to the effect, "Cool it, it's only a bunch of kids."

Q. Now how did he make this comment?
A. On the radio, and I was in the car with the radio on so I overheard this conversation.
Q. And would this conversation being on the radio be general to all RCMP cars in the area?
A. Certainly.

Sergeant Evanoff said he first learned who had fired the shot on the morning of the 11th of October, after he had returned from examining the car and some of the men from Mac-Dowall had returned to the office. He said he was wondering who had fired the shot. At that time Constable Griffiths overheard his conversation and said, "Well, I believe that Constable Bezzola fired a shot."

Sergeant Evanoff said he was satisfied that only one shot was fired.

The bias of at least one member of the jury is clearly reflected in questions he asked following Staff Sergeant Evanoff's testimony:

Juryman: Sergeant Evanoff, there's just one point I find of interest referring to photograph No. 16 indicating that bullet hole or hole in the front of the car — Sergeant Evanoff, with your experience with fire-arms would you not agree that that was well-directed shot at the tire?

Evanoff: I would say, sir, that the shot was directly lined with the tire.

Juryman: As indicated here it would have struck the upper part of the tire had it been another two or three feet forward of that?

Evanoff: Two or three feet forward he would have hit the top of the tire.

Juryman: And taking into consideration the speed and the erratic manner in which this car was being driven — 80 to a hundred miles an hour — that the shot was well directed?

Evanoff: Yes, sir.

The hole was actually very close to the driver's door and several of the officers in their testimony referred to it as being "through the door."

The evidence of Dr. Harry Emson, the pathologist, indicated that the deceased boy had died of a bullet wound in the heart. There were also wounds in the region of the left thigh with fragments of a bullet in them. Dr. Emson said that the mass of metal resembling a bullet that he removed from the chest was very distorted and not identifiable as any particular type of bullet. "It was a mass of metal resembling lead and about the size of the end joint of my thumb or index finger." When asked by Mr. Caldwell if, in his opinion, the leg wounds and the wounds in the upper torso could have represented the by-products of one bullet which was split into pieces upon hitting some object before the body, Dr. Emson replied, "this is one possible interpretation." When asked if he found any indication that more than one bullet struck the body, he replied:

> I can't say. I cannot say whether the mass I recovered from the right chest is the core of a rifle bullet or whether it represents a portion of another bullet such as a solid lead slug from an automatic revolver.

According to Sergeant Evanoff's testimony, the original statements of the juveniles who were occupants of the car indicated that "shots" had been fired at them. In a phone call to Sergeant Evanoff, Dr. Fogel the coroner, similarly stated that the pathologist had indicated that there was some possibility of "bullets" or bullet wounds. Testimony revealed that at least three of the officers at the scene—RCMP constables Griffiths and Federowich and Saskatoon City Policeman Mac-Donald—had revolvers drawn at the time of the shooting. Inasmuch as two of the youths testified to a shot breaking the window, isn't it possible that one bullet through the window hit Muskego in the heart and a second rifle shot hit his leg, and that the remainder of this shot was what one youth heard hitting his door on the other side of the car? The main evidence against this interpretation is a photograph of the driver's side of the car, taken by the RCMP on October 11, showing the window with the frost shield intact.

According to the "one shot" interpretation of the RCMP, the projectile of the probe that was inserted in the hole in the car showed that if Muskego had been slouched over, pieces of the same fragmented bullet could have lodged in his heart and hit his thigh. However, this is a most unlikely position for a driver, allegedly travelling 90 to 100 miles per hour around an RCMP roadblock, to be sitting in. Nevertheless, no one at the inquest suggested any alternative explanation.

Staff Sergeant Kirby, the firearms expert who testified at the inquest, stated that is was more "reasonable to presume" that the lead and copper pieces which he identified were part of one military bullet rather than of a series of bullets, but again, no one asked him why that was a more reasonable presumption. He said he found no evidence to suggest that the lead and copper were the by-products of more than one bullet. In describing the lead portion which penetrated the heart, he said it weighed approximately 49 grains, which is 9 grains more than a .22 calibre long rifle bullet weighs, "so it would have sufficient energy to penetrate a body."

After being directed by the corner, the jury retired at 1:10 P.M. on October 27 and returned at 3:15 P.M. Their verdict, a complete endorsement of the police action, was as follows:

A high powered rifle, the property of the Royal Canadian Mounted Police and in the hands of RCMP Constable John Bezzola was discharged at the speeding car intended at puncturing the left front tire and so disabling the vehicle; possibly due to speed and erratic movement of the car, the bullet discharged from the rifle struck the left front fender panel fragmenting into the interior of the car thus resulting in fatal injury to the deceased.

In considering all the circumstances the police action was at all times properly exercised and good judgement used. Particularly we find the action of Constable Bezzola justifiable. We, the jury attach no blame to any of the authorities involved.

This inquest and this verdict leave curious citizens with a number of unanswered questions.

The police knew all the time that the car had nothing to do with the Robertson affair. By the simplest logic, why would Robertson be speeding towards Saskatoon in the direction of MacDowall, the day after he was alleged to have shot two police officers at MacDowall? In fact, the officers admitted that they knew that the occupants of the car were kids. Staff sergeant Edmondson's evidence to that effect was quite plain. Given this information, why did the RCMP use firearms at all?

The officers stated that they were not prepared to block the roadway completely because they did not wish to cause the car to collide, which might result in the death of all the occupants, but that they did wish to prevent it from getting into the city and as a last resort they were prepared to shoot. Constable Bezzola testified that he would have shot into the radiator of the car if he had not been worried about the danger to other persons as a result of a possible richochet, but that on that account he desisted. Instead, as the car drew alongside him, he fired his rifle at the tire from a distance of 12 feet. If it was his intention to hit the tire and not the occupant, why didn't he use a shotgun? With a shotgun, he would be much surer of hitting the tire, in fact, he could virtually not miss. Considering that Bezzola, according to his classification in the Force, was an expert marksman, it is hard to understand first, how he could have made such an error in judgement as to the choice of weapon and secondly, having elected to use a rifle, how he could have missed and caused the death of Muskego.

Why did no police officer report that Muskego had been killed by a bullet, and not by accident, until the bullet wound was discovered by the pathologist? Why did Constable Bezzola not wait around long enough to report to his superior officer the fact that he had fired the gun? Is it not mandatory for officers of the RCMP to report the use of firearms immediately? Why did no other officer testify conclusively that he had seen Bezzola fire a bullet at the car? And, why was Sergeant Evanoff, who was in charge of the operation, not aware that the shot had been fired?

When the Saskatoon *Star-Phoenix* acquired knowledge of the incident, why did the RCMP attempt to conceal their reasons for firing at the car, first by saying that their officers believed the driver might be Robertson, and then by changing their story when it became apparent that the officers knew all along that it was not Robertson?

Is it possible that the RCMP overreacted due to the fact that two of their members had recently been killed allegedly by Wilfred Stanley Robertson in the MacDowall district and accordingly were shooting at all violators of all laws? If so, can we say that such a police force was acting reasonably and conscientiously? If they had wished to stop the car at all costs, as they said, why didn't they completely block the road at the overpast, which would have made it impossible for the car to have got past? Would it not have been safer to block the road than to shoot at the tire of a car allegedly going 90 miles per hour if the prime concern was not to kill all the occupants? The very fact that the three surviving teenagers were only slightly hurt indicates in the first place that the car was probably not travelling at a speed of from 90 to 100 miles per hour.

Why did the RCMP hand-pick the coroner's jury and name a foreman of the jury a former member of the Force?

Did the jury consider it "good judgement" on the part of the RCMP to pursue teenagers in a car at speeds up to 100 miles an hour, thus endangering their own lives and the lives of anyone else who might have been on that road, particularly when arrangements for roadblocks had been made anyway?

Of the 21 witnesses at the inquest, 13 were members of the RCMP, one was a former member of the RCMP, three were members of the Saskatoon City Police, one was the pathologist, and three were the surviving youths. Why were the drivers of the semi-trailers, who must have been present at the scene, not called as witnesses?

Cases like this raise the serious question of the RCMP's preponderant role in the presentation of evidence. The RCMP investigate the incident; RCMP photographers take the pictures; the RCMP crime lab analyses the evidence, and RCMP "experts" interpret it.

Was there in fact a second bullet which broke the window as alleged by two of the youths?

No one asked those questions we are asking here now, neither the agent of the attorney-general nor anyone else who was present. The only serious cross-examination which took place during the inquest was cross-examination of the juveniles.

The injustices illustrated in the handling of this case—not just by the RCMP but by other elements of society including the press—are particularly glaring when one makes comparisons with the sensational coverage being given at the same time to the murder of two RCMP officers. Three times the *Star-Phoenix's* front-page banner headline was devoted to the search for Robertson: on October 10, "RCMP Launch Massive Manhunt: Two Officers Dead"; on October 12, "Police Comb Area in Search of Murderer", and on October 13, "Murder Suspect Search Continues."

By comparison, the first mention of the death of Muskego was in an accident report which state that five Saskatchewan residents had been killed in accidents over the weekend. One was described as "an unidentified 15-year-old boy killed in a crash of a stolen car at a roadblock near Saskatoon after police had pursued the car for more than 100 miles." Even after it was discovered that an RCMP officer had shot the boy, only a single-column headline appeared "Boy Shot Before Car Crash" on page 3 of the *Star-Phoenix*. The rest of the report was the official RCMP statement on the matter.

Is the life of a 15-year-old Indian boy not worth as much as that of an RCMP officer? Is the death of Michael Muskego further evidence of the racist attitude that permeates this society? If so, the Muskego case is a serious indictment not only of the RCMP, but of all those citizens who stood idly by, saw it happen, and stayed silent.

Afterword

As long as the RCMP are portrayed as an almost sacred institution which can do no wrong, adverse criticism of them will be interpreted by many people as an unpatriotic, even seditious, act. That in itself is not healthy in any society.

The problem of how to limit the power of the RCMP and the police in general is not an easy one. To begin with, the basic role of the police will not be altered until society as a whole is fundamentally changed, and that is probably not going to happen in the immediate future. In the meantime concerned people must constantly struggle to ensure the protection of politicial liberties and to support those oppressed groups who are demanding that they be accorded at least as many civil rights as the more affluent sections of the population. The history of the RCMP provides conclusive evidence that Canadians cannot afford to be complacent about the maintenance of their civil rights.

When confronting the problem of RCMP abuse of power, those people concerned with civil rights might also remind the politicians that the RCMP are quite unnecessary under our federal system of government. The administration of justice is the constitutional responsibility of the provinces, and all provinces could maintain their own police forces, as Ontario and Quebec do. Under our constitution, all the federal government should require in the way of police forces are a few small specialized policing agencies for purely federal matters. Provincial police forces might be not better than the RCMP in many respects, but at least Canada would not have so much police power centralized in one arrogant, secretive and militaristic organization.

During 1973, when the RCMP are being glorified more than ever before, people cannot be reminded too often that all police forces are at best a necessary evil and that the RCMP may not even be necessary.

Notes

Introduction

1 "Report of the RCMP for the Year Ended September 30, 1920." Sessional Papers. Vol. LVIII, No. 8, 1921, No. 28.
2 *RCMP Act,* Part I, Section 21, Sub-section (2).
3 *Ibid.,* Part II, 25 (a).
4 *Ibid.,* Part II, 28 (2) and (3).
5 *Ibid.,* Part III, Section 46.
6 *Ibid.,* Part II, 25 (j).

Chapter 1

1 Macbeth, R. G. *Policing the Plains.* Toronto: The Musson Book Co. Ltd., 1931.
2 *Ibid.,* p. 8.
3 *RCMP Quarterly,* October, 1961.
4 See especially Myers, Gustavus. *A History of Canadian Wealth.* Toronto: Lewis & Samuel, 1972.
5 Horrall, S. W., "Sir John A. Macdonald and the Mounted Police Force for the Northwest Territories". *Canadian Historical Review,* Vol. LIII, No. 2, June, 1972; and Morgan, E. C. *The North West Mounted Police 1873 - 1883.* Unpublished M.A. thesis, Regina Campus, 1970.
6 Horrall and Morgan, *op. cit.*
7 Horrall, *op. cit.*
8 *Ibid.,* p. 182.
9 *Ibid.,* p. 182.
10 Morgan, *op. cit.,* p. 4.
11 Archibald to secretary of state, quoted in Morgan, *op. cit.,* p. 13.
12 *Ibid.,* p. 13.
13 Robertson Ross Report, quoted in Morgan, *op. cit.,* p. 12.
14 McKeagney to Macdonald, May 1, 1873, quoted in Morgan, *op. cit.,* p. 15.
15 Morgan, *op. cit.,* p. 15.
16 Campbell to Mosris, August 14, 1873, quoted in Morgan, *op. cit.,* p. 21.
17 Macdonald to Dufferin, September 23, 1873, quoted in Morgan, *op. cit.,* p. 21.
18 Morgan, *op. cit.,* p. 39.
19 Ramsey, Jack. "My Case Against the RCMP". *Maclean's,* July, 1972.
20 Morgan, *op. cit.,* p. 79.
21 *Ibid.,* p. 79.

22 E. C. Morgan, *op. cit.*, and Ward, W. T. *Administration of Justice in the North West Territories, 1870 - 87.* Unpublished M.A. thesis, University of Alta., Edmonton, 1966.
23 Annual Report of the NWMP for 1882, quoted in Morgan, *op. cit.*, p. 182.
24 E. D. Clark to Deputy Minister of Justice, August 8, 1874, quoted in Morgan, *op. cit.*, p. 184.
25 Morgan, *op. cit.*, p. 85.
26 *Ibid.*, p. 208.
27 *Ibid.*, p. 190.
28 *Ibid.*, p. 211.
29 Letter to *Manitoba Daily Free Press*, September 19, 1883, quoted in Morgan, *op. cit.*, p. 212.
30 Turner, John Peter. *The North-West Mounted Police 1873 - 1893*, Vol. II. Ottawa: King's Printer, 1950, pp. 518 - 21.
31 *Ibid.*, pp. 519 - 20.
32 *Ibid.*, p. 520.
33 Ward, *op. cit.*, pp. 25 - 6.
34 *Ibid.*, p. 94.
35 G. A. French, "Recalls Earlier Years", *Scarlet and Gold*, 1953, p. 37, quoted in Morgan *op. cit.*, p. 76.
36 Ward, *op. cit.*, p. 98.
37 Howard, J. K. *Strange Empire.* New York: William Morrow and Company, 1952, p. 509.
38 Morton, W. L. "Canada and the Canadian Indians: What went wrong?" *The Quarterly of Canadian Studies*, Vol. 2, No. 1, Spring, 1972, p. 3.
39 Morgan, *op. cit.*, pp. 134 - 5.
40 Fitzpatrick, F. J. E. *Sergeant 331.* New York: published by the author, 1921, pp. 36 - 7.
41 Denny, Sir Cecil E. *The Law Marches West.* Toronto: J. M. Dent and Sons (Canada) Ltd., 1939, p. 226.
42 Turner, *op. cit.*, Vol. II, p. 259.
43 *Ibid.*, p. 260.

Chapter 2

1 Macbeth, R. G. *Policing the Plains.* Toronto: The Musson Book Company Ltd., 1931, pp. 93 - 4.
2 Turner, John P. *The North-West Mounted Police 1873 - 1893.* Vol. II. Ottawa: King's Printer, 1950, p. 7.
3 For accounts of the strike see:
    Morgan, E. C. *The North West Mounted Police 1873 - 1883.* Unpublished M.A. thesis, Regina Campus, 1970, pp. 158 - 161; and
    Manitoba Daily Free Press, Dec. 17 - 27, 1883.
4 *Free Press*, Dec. 18, 1883.
5 *Ibid.*, Dec. 24, 1883.
6 Fitzpatrick, F. J. E. *Sergeant 331.* New York: published by the author, 1921, pp. 110 - 1.
7 *Ibid.*, p. 111.
8 *Ibid.*, p. 111.
9 Annual Report of NWMP for 1883, quoted in Morgan, *op. cit.*, pp. 159 - 60.

10   *Ibid.*, pp. 159 - 60.
11   Superintendent Egan to Commissioner Irvine, quoted in
       Annual Report of the NWMP, 1883, and in Morgan
       op. cit., p. 161.
12   Quoted in Morgan, *op. cit.*, p. 160.
13   Steele, Colonel Sam. *Forty Years In Canada*. Winnipeg:
       Russell Long and Co., 1914, pp. 196 - 201.
14   *Ibid.*, p. 197.
15   *Ibid.*, p. 201.
16   Myers, Gustavus. *A History of Canadian Wealth*. Toronto:
       James Lewis and Samuel, 1972, pp. 126 - 31.

Chapter 3

1   Graham, Roger. *Arthur Meighen*. Toronto: Clark Irwin &
      Company, 1960, Vol. 1, p. 138.
2   Annual Report on Labour Organization in Canada, 1917,
      cited in Lipton, Charles. *The Trade Union Movement of
      Canada 1827 - 1959*. Canadian Social Publications Ltd.,
      1968, p. 175.
3   Phillips, Paul. *No Power Greater*. Vancouver: B.C. Federation
      of Labour, Boag Foundation, 1967, pp. 72 - 5.
4   *Ibid.*, pp. 73 - 4.
5   Annual Report of RNWMP for year ending Sept. 30, 1918.
      Sessional Paper No. 28, 1919.
6   Robin, Martin. *Radical Politics and Canadian Labour 1880 -
      1930*. Kingston: Industrial Relations Centre, Queen's Uni-
      versity, 1968, pp. 164 - 8.
7   C. H. Cahan to D. J. Doherty, Sept. 14, 1918, *Borden Papers*.
      Public Archives of Canada, cited in Robin, *op. cit.*, p. 165.
8   Robin, *op. cit.*, pp. 165 - 167.
9   Accounts of the Winnipeg General Strike are included in the
      following:
      D. G. Masters. *The Winnipeg General Strike*. Toronto: U. of
      T. Press, 1950.
      Robin, Martin. *Radical Politics and Canadian Labour*. King-
      ston: Industrial Relations Centre, Queen's University, 1968.
      McNaught, Kenneth. *A Prophet in Politics*. Toronto: U. of T.
      Press, 1959.
      Lipton, Charles. *The Trade Union Movement of Canada 1827 -
      1959*. Canadian Social Publications Ltd., 1968.
      Jamieson, Stuart. *Times of Trouble: Labour Unrest and In-
      dustrial Conflict in Canada, 1900 - 66*. Ottawa: Information
      Canada, 1971.
10   Minutes of the Executive of the Saskatchewan Grain Growers'
       Association, May 21, 1919. p. 111. Cited in Masters, D. C.
       The Winnipeg General Strike. Toronto: U. of T. Press,
       1950, p. 71.
11   Gideon Robertson in a telegram to the Federal Cabinet,
       May 25, 1919. Cited in Masters, *op. cit.*, p. 78.
12   Masters, *op. cit.*, p. 104.
13   *Ibid.*, p. 77.
14   *Ibid.*, p. 77
15   Robin, *op. cit.*, p. 181.

16 Masters, *op. cit.*, pp. 105 - 6.
17 *Ibid.*, p. 87.
18 Annual Report of the RNWMP for year ending September 30, 1919, p. 12.
19 Lipton, *op. cit.*, p. 199.
20 Kelly, Nora. *The Men of the Mounted.* Toronto and Vancouver: J. M. Dent and Sons (Canada) Ltd., 1949, p. 204.
21 Annual Report of the RNWMP for year ending September 30, 1919.
22 *Canadian Annual Review*, 1920, p. 467.
23 Annual Report of RNWMP for year ending September 30, 1919. See Appendix of this book.
24 Jamieson, Stuart. *Times of Trouble: Labour Unrest and Industrial Conflict in Canada, 1900 - 66.* Study No. 22 for Task Force on Labour Relations. Ottawa: Information Canada, 1971.
25 Phillips, Alan. *The Living Legend.* Toronto and Boston: Little, Brown and Company, 1954, p. 86.

Chapter 4

1 House of Commons. *Debates.* Ottawa: April 4, 1922, p. 670.
2 *Ibid.*, p. 672.
3 *Ibid.*, p. 672. See also the Appendix.
4 *Ibid.*, p. 670.
5 See Scott, F. R. "The Trial of the Toronto Communists." Kingston: *Queen's Quarterly*, 1932, p. 514.
6 *Ibid.*, p. 512.
7 Jamieson, Stuart. *Times of Trouble: Labour Unrest and Industrial Conflict in Canada, 1900 - 66*, Task Force on Labour Relations Study No. 22. Ottawa: Information Canada, 1971, pp. 235 - 6.
    Also, Price, W. H. *Agents of Revolution.* "A History of the Workers' Unity League, Setting forth its Origins and Aims." Public Archives of Canada. Ottawa: *Bennett Papers.* M-1314, Film No. 300, pp. 388406 - 24.
8 "RCMP Annual Relport for the Year Ending September 30, 1932", p. 69.
9 Saskatoon *Star-Phoenix*, September 21, 1933. Also Lorne Brown, "Unemployment Relief Camps in Saskatchewan, 1933 - 36." *Saskatchewan History.* Saskatoon: Autumn, 1970, p. 88.
10 Letter from M. A. MacPherson to R. B. Bennett. Public Archives of Canada. Ottawa: *Bennett Papers,* Microfilm pages 495029 - 30. February 12, 1934. Also Lorne Brown, *op. cit.*, pp. 97 - 98.
11 Letter from Brigadier General Alex Ross to Hon. W. A. Gordon. Public Archives of Canada. Ottawa: *McNaughton Papers,* Vol. 48, 331A. April 27, 1933.
12 Letter from W. A. Gordon to McNaughton. Public Archives of Canada. Ottawa: *McNaughton Papers,* Vol. 48, 331A. May 2, 1933.
13 *Debates, op. cit.*, April 4, 1922, p. 673.

Chapter 5

1 Lower, Arthur. "Is the RCMP a Threat to Our Liberty?" *Maclean's*, July 6, 1957, p. 57.
2 House of Commons *Debates*. Public Archives of Canada. Ottawa: March 23, 1932, p. 1412.
3 Bennett to R. B. Hanson, M.P., October 22, 1931. Public Archives of Canada. Ottawa: *Bennett Papers*, M - 1453, Vol. 798, Roll 394, p. 493597.
4 Public statement by Perley, April 26, 1935. Public Archives of Canada. Ottawa: *Bennett Papers*, File No. U - 125, Jan. - April, 1935, p. 495791.
5 Jamieson, Stuart. *Times of Trouble: Labour Unrest and Industrial Conflict in Canada, 1900 - 66*. Task Force on Labour Relations Study No. 22. Ottawa: Information Canada, pp. 214 - 5.
6 Toronto *Mail and Empire*, Feb. 5, 1931.
7 *Ibid.*
8 *Empire Club of Canada*, Addresses Delivered to the Members During the Year 1933 - 34. Toronto: Printer's Guild, Limited, 1934, p. 418.
9 *Western Producer*, April 21, 1932.
10 "Fascism A La Canadienne", *Canadian Forum*, May, 1932, p. 284, quotations from *Mail and Empire*.
11 "Fascism A La Canadienne", *Canadian Forum*, May, 1932, p. 284.
12 *Debates, op. cit.*, 1932, Vol. iii, pp. 2658 - 9, 2683 - 8, 2716.
13 *Ibid.*, p. 2683.
14 Secret Memo of Chief of the General Staff to the Adjutant-General, October 14, 1931. Public Archives of Canada. Ottawa: *McNaughton Papers*, Vol. 10, File 46.
15 *Canadian Forum*, February, 1935, p. 165.
16 Jamieson, *op. cit.*, p. 237.
17 Confidential Memo signed by McNaughton and distributed to Adjutant-General, Quartermaster-General, D.O.C., M.D. No. 11, Deputy Minister of Labour, Prime Minister's Secretary, and Commissioner of the RCMP, May 29, 1935. Public Archives of Canada. *Department of Defence Papers*.
18 *Ibid.*
19 Letter from Lockwood to Bennett, June 26, 1935. Letter from Bennett to Lockwood, July 8, 1935. Public Archives of Canada. Ottawa: *Bennett Papers*, M - 989, Film No. 83.
20 See Appendix.
21 Jamieson, *op. cit.*, p. 221.
22 *Ibid.*, p. 221.
23 Hanson, S. D. *The Estevan Strike and Riot, 1931*. Unpublished M. A. thesis, University of Saskatchewan Regina Campus, 1971, p. 122.
24 *Ibid.*, p. 156.
25 *Ibid.*, p. 157.
26 *Ibid.*, pp. 128 - 63.
27 *Ibid.*, p. 136.
28 *Ibid.*, p. 138.

29 *Estevan Mercury*, March 10, 1932, quoted in Hanson, *op. cit.*, p. 142.
30 Hanson, *op. cit.*, p. 142.
31 *Canadian Labor Defender*, March, 1932, quoted in Hanson, *op. cit.*, p. 128.
32 *Leader-Post*, Oct. 13, 1931, quoted in Hanson, *op. cit.*, p. 138.
33 Hanson, *op. cit.*, p. 139.
34 *Ibid.*, pp. 159 - 60.
35 *Ibid.*, p. 160.
36 Wylie Commission Proceedings, p. 217, quoted in Hanson, *op. cit.*, p. 127.
37 See other examples in Jamieson, *op. cit.*, and Phillips, Paul. *No Power Greater*. Vancouver: B. C. Federation of Labour, 1967.
38 See the following for discussions of the camps:
   Liversedge, Ronald. *Reflections of the On-to-Ottawa Trek*. (Mimeographed booklet privately distributed.)
   Gray, James. *The Winter Years*. Toronto: MacMillan of Canada, 1966.
   Brown, Lorne. "Unemployment Relief Camps in Saskatchewan 1933 - 36". *Saskatchewan History*. Saskatoon: Autumn, 1970. "The Trek to Ottawa, 1935, Remembered." *Canadian Dimension*. Winnipeg: June, 1971.
39 Brown, Lorne. "The Trek to Ottawa, 1935, Remembered." *Canadian Dimension*. Winnipeg: June, 1971, p. 57.
40 Swettenham, John. *McNaughton*, Vol. I. Toronto: Ryerson Press, 1968, p. 280.
41 For accounts of the riot see Jamieson, *op. cit.* and Appendix.
42 Jamieson, *op. cit.*, p. 269.

Chapter 6

(there are no notes for Chapter 6)

Chapter 7

1 Reuben, William A. *The Atom Spy Hoax*. N.Y.: Action Books, 1955, p. 38.
2 Sandwell, B. K. *The Nation*, May 4, 1946, quoted in Reuben, *op. cit.*, p. 37.
3 *Ibid.*, p. 38.
4 *Ibid.*, p. 39.
5 Royal Commissioners' Report, quoted in Reuben, *op. cit.*, p. 39.
6 Reuben, *op. cit.*, p. 39.
7 Fraser, Blair. "Can McCarthy Happen Here." *Maclean's*. Toronto: March 15, 1954, p. 76.
8 Katz, Sidney. "Inside Canada's Secret Police." *Maclean's*. Toronto: April 20, 1963. Also Blair Fraser's Column, *Maclean's*, Jan. 15, 1952.
9 Blair Fraser's column, *op. cit.*, Jan. 15, 1952, pp. 5, 44.
10 Katz, *op. cit.*, p. 39.
11 Blair Fraser's column, *op. cit.*, Jan. 15, 1952, pp. 5, 44.
12 Katz, *op. cit.*, pp. 14, 39, 40.

13 Royal Canadian Mounted Police. *Law and Order in Canadian Democracy*. Ottawa: Queen's Printer, 1952, p. vii.

14 *Ibid.,* p. 1.

15 *Ibid.,* p. 160.

16 *Ibid.,* pp. 166 - 67.

17 *Ibid.,* p. 154.

18 *Ibid.,* p. 155.

19 Speech of George McClellan in the *RCMP Quarterly,* Oct., 1961.

20 Speech of Commissioner C. W. Harvison in the *RCMP Quarterly,* Jan., 1962.

21 "The Path of Democratic Justice." Speech by J. Edgar Hoover to 1960 Annual Conference of International Associations of Chiefs of Police. *RCMP Quarterly,* Jan., 1961, p. 188.

22 *Ibid.,* p. 188.

Chapter 8

1 Katz, Sidney. "Inside Canada's Secret Police." *Maclean's.* Toronto: April 20, 1963, p. 34.

2 *Ibid.,* p. 37.

3 House of Commons *Debates,* Ottawa: June 3, 1963, p. 590.

4 Katz, *op. cit.,* p. 37.

5 "Proposed Resolution Concerning RCMP Activity on Campus." *CAUT Bulletin.* Ottawa: The Canadian Association of University Teachers, November, 1962, p. 30.

6 "The RCMP on the Campus." *CAUT Bulletin.* Ottawa: April, 1963, p. 28.

7 House of Commons *Debates, op. cit.,* June 3, 1963, p. 590.

8 *Debates, op. cit.,* December 14, 1962, pp. 2664 - 5.

9 *Debates, op. cit.,* January 21, 1963, p. 2920.

10 Katz, *op. cit.,* pp. 14 - 5.

11 "The RCMP on the Campus", *op. cit.,* April, 1963, p. 28.

12 *The Gateway.* Edmonton: The University of Alberta Students' Council, March 27, 1963, quoted in House of Commons *Debates,* May 31, 1963, p. 513.

13 *Ibid.,* p. 513.

14 *Ibid.,* p. 513.

15 *Debates, op. cit.,* June 3, 1963, p. 584.

16 *Debates, op. cit.,* May 31, 1963, p. 513.

17 "Memorandum Concerning RCMP Activities on University Campuses." April, 1964, pp. 36 - 41.

18 *Ibid.* pp. 36 - 41.

19 *Debates, op. cit.,* December 4, 1963, p. 5411.

20 *Debates, op. cit.,* November 28, 1963, p. 5206 - 13.

21 *Ibid.,* p. 5213.

22 "National Security and the University." *CAUT Bulletin.* December, 1967, p. 14, citing *Hansard,* July 2, 1964.

23 *Ibid.,* p. 23.

24 *Report of the Royal Commission on Security* (Abridged). Ottawa: The Queen's Printer, June, 1969, p. 1.

25 *Ibid.,* pp. 8, 9.

26 *Ibid.,* p. 8.

27 *Ibid.,* p. 6.

28 *Ibid.*, p. 45.
29 *Ibid.*, p. 45.
30 *Ibid.*, p. 23.
31 *Ibid.*, p. 24.
32 *Debates, op. cit.*, June 26, 1969, p. 10, 636.
33 *Ibid.*, p. 10, 637.
34 See *Quebec: A Chronicle 1968 - 1972*, edited by Robert Chodos and Nick Auf Der Maur. Toronto: James Lewis and Samuel, Publishers, 1972.
35 *Debates., op. cit.*, February 17, 1969, p. 5590.
36 "Our policy on deserters 'unjust', minister says." Toronto *Star*. Toronto: February 21, 1969.
37 *Ibid.*
38 *Ibid.*
39 "Remove the barriers to U.S. 'refugees'." Toronto *Star*. Toronto: May 7, 1969. Editorial.
40 Clarkson, Stephen. "Wanted: A liberal policy on political immigrants from the United States." Toronto *Star*, May 7, 1969.
41 "Immigration Officer Testifies That Three U.S. Deserters Had Entered Canada Illegally." *Globe and Mail*. Toronto: April 1, 1970.
42 *Ibid.*
43 *Ibid.*
44 "Conspiracy is charged in deserter inquiry." Canadian Press story in Ottawa *Citizen*. Ottawa: April 14, 1970.
45 *Ibid.*
46 Sagi, Douglas. "Inquiry is told of deportations of Americans." *Globe and Mail*. Toronto: April 14, 1970.
47 Sagi, Douglas. "Immigration men called in RCMP, inquiry is told." *Globe and Mail*. Toronto: March 25, 1970.
48 *Ibid.*
49 Sagi, Douglas. "RCMP constable tells inquiry he forgot rule on deportation." *Globe and Mail*. Toronto: March 26, 1970.
50 Canadian Press story on Stewart Report, *Globe and Mail*. Toronto: June 26, 1970.
51 *Ibid.*
52 *Ibid.*
53 *Ibid.*
54 *Ibid.*
55 Crook, Farrell. "Man deported to U.S. despite appeal rights." *Globe and Mail*. Toronto: Oct. 24, 1972.
56 McNeil, Gerard. "RCMP may resume campus surveillance." Canadian Press story carried in Regina *Leader Post*, May 4, 1971.
57 *Ibid.*
58 *Ibid.*
59 *Ibid.*
60 Maeots, Krista. "The Children, the Mounties and questions." Ottawa *Citizen*. Ottawa: April 4, 1970.
61 Maeots, Krista. "Deserters, immigrants equal." Ottawa *Citizen*. Ottawa: April 8, 1970.
62 Interview with Roy Atkinson.

63 Schmidt, John. "Agricultural Alberta." Calgary *Herald*. Calgary: June 14, 1972, regular column.
64 Interview with Fred Gudmundson, Director of Organization and Education for the NFU.
65 Schmidt, *op. cit.*, June 14, 1972.
66 *Ibid.*, June 15, 1972.
67 Katz, *op. cit.*, p. 35.
68 Interview with Roy Atkinson.
69 Interview with Roy Atkinson.
70 Interview with Roy Atkinson.
71 "Campus Disturbances Linked to Agitators from U.S., RCMP says." Canadian Press story appearing in *Globe and Mail*. Toronto: May 7, 1969.
72 *Ibid.*
73 Kelly, William H. "Spying in Canada: a special report by an RCMP expert." *Canadian Magazine*, November 29, 1969, p. 6.
74 McNeil, Gerard. "RCMP may resume campus surveillance." Canadian Press story carried in the Regina *Leader Post*, May 4, 1971.
75 Katz, Sidney, *op. cit.*, p. 40.
76 Macdonald, W. E. G. Editor of *Scarlet and Gold*. Editorial in *Scarlet and Gold*, 1970, p. 34.
77 *Ibid.*, p. 34.
78 Macdonald, W.E.G. "A New Image for Policemen." *Scarlet and Gold*, 1971, p. 19.

Chapter 9

1 Newman, Peter C. "Inside the RCMP: the conscience of a good cop." *Maclean's*. Toronto: July, 1972, p. 1.
2 Statutes of Canada, 38 Victoria, Ch. 50, Section 22, quoted in Morgan, E. C. *The North-West Mounted Police 1873-1883*. Unpublished M.A. thesis, Regina Campus, 1970, p. 213.
3 Hanson, S. D. *The Estevan Strike and Riot, 1931*. Unpublished M.A. thesis, Regina Campus, 1971, p. 246.
4 Fetherstonhaugh, R. C. *The Royal Canadian Mounted Police*. New York: Corrick and Evans Inc., 1938, p. XI.
5 Kelly, Nora. *The Men of the Mounted*. Toronto-Vancouver: J. M. Dent and Sons (Canada) Ltd., 1949, Acknowledgements.
6 Phillips, Alan. *The Living Legend*. Boston-Toronto: Little, Brown and Co., 1954, Dedication.
7 *Ibid.*, p. 101.
8 *Ibid.*, p. 102.
9 Fetherstonhaugh, *op. cit.*, p. 287.
10 Bette, Constable F. J. "Citizenship Ceremony at Prince George, B.C." *RCMP Quarterly*, October, 1951, pp. 138 - 9.
11 Kelly, W. H. "Youth and the Police." *RCMP Quarterly*, July, 1946, p. 34.
12 *RCMP Quarterly*, October, 1946, p. 143.
13 *Scarlet and Gold*, 1969, p. 6.
14 *Scarlet and Gold*, 1969, p. 27.

15 *Scarlet and Gold*, 1968, p. 25.
16 Bronfman, Samuel. "Neighbours in Democracy — Canada and the United States". *Scarlet and Gold*, 1968, p. 31.
17 *RCMP Quarterly*. "Canadian Chiefs of Police Conference." Jan., 1961, p. 198.
18 RCMP Supt. E. A. F. Holm, Victoria, B.C., Oct. 19, 1968. Carried in *Scarlet and Gold*, 1968, p. 45.
19 Editorial, *Scarlet and Gold*, 1968, p. 45.
20 Sask. Education Minister Gordon MacMurchy, Nov. 21, 1972. See Appendix.
21 Steward, Hartley. "Mounties are Fun." *Canadian Magazine*, January 27, 1973, p. 2.

Chapter 10

1   McDowell, Stanley. "Minister denies teenagers paid for police tips." Toronto: *Globe and Mail*, August 16, 1971, p. 1.
2   McDowell, Stanley. "Goyer Orders RCMP's Higgitt to prove charges 18-yr-old informer intimidated." Toronto: *Globe and Mail*, Sept. 10, 1971, p. 1.
3   Ottawa (CP). "RCMP to probe informer's claim." *Leader Post*, Regina: Sept. 10, 1971.
4   McDowell, *op. cit.*, "Goyer Orders . . .", p. 1.
5   Carriere, Vianney. "Stop paying youths for information Goyer tells RCMP." Toronto: *Globe and Mail*, Sept. 18, 1971, p. 1.
6   *Ibid.*, p. 1.
7   Goyer's statement to the House of Commons. Ottawa (CP). "RCMP policy on juveniles outlined." *Leader Post*. Regina: September 17, 1971, p. 1.
8   Ramsay, Jack. "My Case Against the RCMP." *Maclean's*. Toronto: July, 1972, p. 65.
9   Ottawa (CP). "Number of Indians in jail said alarming." *Leader Post*. Regina: March 2, 1972, p. 32.
10 *Ibid.*, p. 32.
11 Report to the Attorney-General of Saskatchewan from two members of his department investigating allegations by residents of Sandy Bay. Musk, Charles E. and MacKay, Kenneth W. "Summary of the Sandy Bay Investigation." Regina: April 23, 1972, to April 25, 1972.
12 *Ibid.*, p. 5.
13 *Special to the Globe and Mail* (Prince Albert). "RCMP harassing Indians, committing sexual offences against women, head of group charges." *Globe and Mail*, January 13, 1973, p. 11.
14 Press Release of the Metis Society of Saskatchewan, July 7, 1972. Verified by the transcript of the court proceedings in the case. Needless to say, the contents of the press release were not picked up by the regular press.
15 Letter from Myron A. Kuziak, lawyer for the M.S.S., to the Hon. R. J. Romanow, Attorney-General of Saskatchewan, June 20, 1972.
16 Report from Serje Kujawa, Director of Public Prosecutions (Sask.) to the Attorney-General. July 4, 1972.
17 *Globe and Mail, op. cit.*, January 13, 1973.

18 *The Liquor Act,* Saskatchewan, Section 101, Sub-section (4).

Chapter 11

1 "The Case of Fred Quilt." Pamphlet produced by voluntary
   labor under the auspices of the Fred Quilt Committee.
2 *Ibid.*
3 Odam, Jes. "Trial demanded for constable Quilt inquest
   verdict 'not enough'." *Vancouver Sun.* Vancouver: Aug.
   4, 1971, p. 1. Unlike the cases in Saskatchewan involving
   Indians and Metis which we deal with in this book, the
   Quilt case in B.C. did receive a great deal of publicity
   from the media.
4 "The Case of Fred Quilt," *op. cit.*
5 *Ibid.*
6 Ramsay, Jack. "My Case Against the RCMP." *Maclean's.*
   Toronto: July, 1972, p. 58.

Chapter 12

(No notes for chapter 12)

About the Authors

Lorne Brown lectures in political science at the University of Saskatchewan in Regina. Caroline Brown is a researcher at CBC Regina.